My Daddy and Me

Stories and Poems

By
The Late Joseph DeStasio-Senior
and
Eileen DiStasio-Clark

Table of Contents

Dedication

With Great Love and Appreciation to

those who Have and Do Bless My Life.

My Family:

Joseph DeStasio Sr. & Miriam Lucille Baragone DeStasio

My Late Parents,

Andrea Jean DeStasio McIntosh

My Older Sister and Their Families,

Joseph DeStasio Jr.

My Younger and Only Brother and Their Families,

Donna Marie DeStasio Wagner

My Younger Sister and Their Families,

My Children,

Eileen, Rebekah, Rachel,

S. Michael, Jennifer, Sharon, Tara,

Stephanie, Apryll, Mikaelah, & M. Trevor

and

THEIR Families!!

Acknowledgement

First and foremost, I deeply express my sincere gratitude to our Heavenly Father for blessing me with the gift and talent of writing! I know I could not do what I do without His assistance.

I also want to acknowledge and express gratitude to the members of my birth family—Joseph Sr., Miriam, Andrea, Joseph Junior, and Donna. All the experiences of my childhood years, experiences that taught me so very much and enabled me to reveal my true self to myself, came about through my experiences and relationships with them.

And, of course, it goes without saying, but I will say it anyway: I also want to acknowledge and note my gratitude to my children, Eileen, Rebekah, Rachel, S. Michael, Jennifer, Sharon, Tara, Stephanie, Apryll, Mikaelah, and M. Trevor, and their families! Through multiple things they said to me over multiple years, I finally came to the realization that Heavenly Father gave me the gift of writing and opened the doors to these experiences because He knew that by sharing them with others, others could feel His love, too. And He definitely wants us all to know that He, Heavenly Father, Heavenly Mother, and Jehovah truly do loves us!!!

About the Author

Eileen DiStasio-Clark was born on September 6, 1953, in West Reading, Pennsylvania to Joseph and Miriam DeStasio. She is the second oldest of four children; her siblings being Andrea McIntosh, Joseph DeStasio Junior, and Donna Wagner. Eileen now lives in Missouri, and is the mother of 11 children— 9 girls and 2 boys: Eileen, Rebekah, Rachel, S. Michael, Jennifer, Sharon, Tara, Stephanie, Apryll, Mikaelah, and M. Trevor. As a member of The Church of Jesus Christ of Latter-Day Saints, she has served in various positions, teaching, leading, and ministering to children, youth, and adults. Eileen established, and is the President/Director of Pursuit of Excellence Institute of Family Education, a non-profit organization focused on the family. Presently, she holds an AA, a BA, and an MA in Clinical Psychology and is working on the completion of her Doctoral degree.

Introduction

My father, who passed from this life in November of 2014, and I, who am still here, had a relationship that was closer than crossed fingers. He was my best friend, my exemplar, and my inspiration in many ways. So important was he to me, and still is, that I once wrote this to express all of that:

My Dad's Example

My Dad was a 5'5" Giant!

He was a quiet man, a gentle man, a kind and humble man.

He was an angel on Earth!

He never sought for riches; he gave all he could and more.

He lived simply, loved greatly, gave generously,

and set, by the way he lived a noble example!

The advice personified by that example is this…

Love God Above All Else! Live First For Family!

Work Hard! Play Fair! Make Life Simple!

Be Humble! Be Kind! Be Gentle!

Be Generous! Be Genuine!

And Always…

Make God's Will Your will!!

Now, with all that said, well, printed, there should be no wonder why we did everything together, and one of the things we both enjoyed doing together was writing. My dad wrote poems, songs, stories, and talks, and so did I. Herein are some of the poems, songs, stories, and talks that survived the years, the moves, and the changes that life put in our paths.

Some he wrote. Some I wrote. Some we wrote together!

So now, read and enjoy!!

OH! One more thing!

The poem, "If You Would Let Me Teach You," which is inserted between the poems "Sad Day Sonnett" and "Silence Is Not Always Golden," is a poem I wrote on February 2, 2007, with the hopes of beginning, able to share with a friend, who was one of my college instructors at that time, a bit of our Heavenly Parent's True Gospel that was brought to us through Jesus the Christ.

Because I wanted to share as much as I could, the poem grew to 120 verses. Now, because there are many topics addressed, I decided to divide the original poem into 10 sections, with each section identified by its subtitle.

Okay, now that all that is said,

Read and Enjoy!

Stories from My Daddy and Me
Dreaming of Success

By
Joseph DeStasio Sr.

Undated

One day, a man walked into a psychiatrist's office, and boy, did he look bad! He was ashen grey, like death warmed over, and he was shaking all over. His eyes were sunken deep into his head. There were dark circles under the circles under his eyes. He hadn't slept in months! He begged the doctor to help him!

The man told the psychiatrist about a recurring dream he had been having. Every time he'd fall asleep, he'd have the same frightening nightmare. There he was, just walking down the street. He'd go right up to this building, come up to this huge door, and then, no matter what he did, he could never open the door to get inside.

He'd push and strain against the door. Nothing! It wouldn't budge an inch. No matter how hard he struggled, no matter what super human strength he sought to muster, nothing! He simply couldn't get in.

He would wake up in a cold sweat, shaking, scared, and exhausted. It was so bad that no matter how tired be became, he was afraid to close his eyes. He said he felt like he was going to die if he didn't get in through that door, and he couldn't!

The doctor asked him why it was so important to open that door, and the man replied that it was the door to his future. He didn't know how he knew that, but this was the door that would lead from failure to success, and he couldn't open it!

The psychiatrist thought for a moment, then asked the man, "You have this dream every time you sleep?"

The man nodded yes.

The doctor said, "Tonight, before you close your eyes, I want you to give yourself the suggestion that when you come to the door again, you're going to notice everything about it, every detail, no matter how insignificant you think it is. Then, come back tomorrow and tell me what you've seen."

The man thanked the doctor listlessly, and though he held out little hope of the advice having any effect, he promised that he would do his best.

When the doctor saw the man the next day, he couldn't believe his eyes! Gone was the shaken, shrunken fellow who had visited his office just the day before. This man looked vibrant and alive; his eyes were bright, and he was smiling! The startled doctor quickly ushered the man into his office for an explanation and asked the man what had happened.

"Before I went to sleep, just like you told me to, I gave myself the suggestion to notice and remember every detail about the Door to Success. So, when I came up to the door, I pushed harder than I ever had before. I strained against it, pushing and pushing. Finally, I stood back and looked at the door. And you know what I saw?"

"No!" said the doctor excitedly. "Tell me! Tell me!"

The man smiled and said, "There was a sign on the door. It said, 'Pull.'"

The End—the Happy End!

Your Head Is Empty

By
Joseph DeStasio Sr.
Sometime after September 1974

Once there was a little girl who decided not to go to church. Her mother asked what was wrong.

"I don't feel well," she said.

The mother, in turn, said, "Honey, you haven't eaten anything; your stomach is empty. If you eat something, you will feel better."

So, the little girl did just that.

When they—the little girl and her family—arrived at church, the little girl noticed one of the other church members speaking to the Bishop.

"How are you feeling?" the man asked the Bishop.

The Bishop replied, "Not too well. I have a headache."

Hearing the Bishop's reply, the little girl approached the Bishop and said, "I know what's wrong with you. Your head is empty."

The End—the Funny End!

I Remember

Joseph DeStasio Sr.
November 10, 1985

The year was 1975. We lived in the suburbs in the borough of West Reading, Pennsylvania. I was an insurance salesman, and trying to find people at home during Christmas week was like trying to find a bargain in a Resort Gift Shop. It was the day before Christmas, and as I was behind schedule in my work, so I decided to work until noon that day.

"Don't forget to pick up a tree!" my wife cried out as I prepared to leave in my usual Dagwood style of departure.

It was only after a flurry of snowflakes patted my face that my mind snapped to reality. After a lickety-split brush off of snow, I entered my car and, as an afterthought, peered through a maze of compounding, glistening crystal-like snowflakes, which had settled on the car window. I looked toward the house and uttered, "I will get a tree."

11

As a child, I was very close to my dad, and every year, to the day he was laid to rest, I helped him pick out our Christmas tree. I have been blessed with a kind, understanding, and loving wife and four of the most beautiful children on this side of heaven, three girls and one boy.

Lost in thought, I failed to notice that the snow had turned to rain. The blast of a horn startled me. I froze at the wheel as I applied the brakes. The car lurched forward. "Good Heavens," I cried out, "what is happening?"

The temperature, being below freezing, quickly set a glass-like sheet of ice on the street. I tried looking out of the windshield and received another shock. It was frosted. The heater hadn't been working. Within the body and shelter of this machine, for the first time in my life, I found myself its prisoner. In a matter of seconds, so many thoughts entered my mind that my head felt like a computer gone haywire. The circuits were all buzzing simultaneously. Finally, as the circuits repaired themselves, I slowly opened the door and peeked out. I got the strangest feeling. There wasn't a car in sight.

I had skidded against the side of a telephone pole, where the car had come to rest, but for the grace of God, I was uninjured, and the car had only a few minor scratches. Although somewhat shaken, I managed to work through noon and returned home around three p.m.

My son and I immediately left in search of a tree. We traveled for two hours. All presentable trees were sold. I was becoming rather desperate.

Suddenly, my son blurted out, "Hey Dad, I know where we might find a tree."

We drove off to Two Guys Department Store, approximately four miles from our home. Due to the lateness of the day, I became somewhat skeptical. However, I did manage a small silent prayer. Upon arrival, my heart skipped a beat. There were few cars on the lot and not a tree in sight.

My son cried out, "Let's go in anyway." And so, we did.

As luck would have it, the few remaining trees were stacked in a corner of the Garden Center. A salesman approached us, and, at this point, I would have paid any price for a tree. My mind reeled as I heard him say, "We are selling out; take your pick, only twenty-five cents a tree."

To this day, I still remember that most beautiful tree!

The End—the Grateful End!

Feeding the Ducks

By
Eileen DiStasio-Clark
Undated

Once upon a time, not too long ago, there was a sweet little girl whom everyone called Elne who, with her older sister, whom everyone called Area, liked to feed the ducks that lived in the creek that ran thought the park that surrounded the museum that was just one mile from their house.

Sometimes they would go to the park with their family, sometimes with just their younger sister or their brother or both of them, sometimes with their cousins, sometimes... well, you know what I am saying. They would go to the park, and whether it was with someone else or just themselves, they would always go there prepared to feed the ducks that lived in the creek.

They took bread, torn into little pieces, or crackers, or cookies their mommy had made that they crumbled up. They would toss the bread, crackers, or crumbled cookies into the water to feed the ducks that were in the creek. They would drop them on the trail or throw them on the grass to feed the ducks that were walking around outside of the creek. Sometimes, when the ducks walked up to them, they would even let the ducks eat the bread, crackers, or cookies right out of their hands. Yes, they really did love to feed the ducks. But that was not all that they did. They also liked to walk the trail!

Side Note: That trail is called Wyomissing Creek Trail because it goes alongside the Wyomissing Creek. And, just in case you were wondering, it is a 2.6-mile-long trail, which Elne and Area usually walked all the way from one end to the other. So, when they took a walk, they took a WALK!

Side Note from the Side Note: That is not what most people would call a very long walk, but for little kids, it was long enough to be a good workout.

Now, back to the other side of the other side.

As they walked, they talked about this, that, everything else, and nothing at all. They looked up at the clouds; they took turns describing what they saw in the clouds. Sometimes they described faces, sometimes horses, sometimes boats, someti— well, you know what I am saying. Because they had amazing imaginations, they saw a lot of different things in the clouds.

They also looked for treasure. Now, real treasure, what people would call real treasure, was not what they found, but what they found was treasure to them, things like coins or toys, or interesting leaves.

Sometimes, they climbed at least one of the trees that lined the trail. But often times, they climbed one tree after another until they got to a tree whose lowest branches were too high for them to reach. When that happened, they just turned around and went back down the trail they had just come up. But they did not walk; they hopped, skipped, jumped, and ran, playing Toe-Tag all the way back.

They even liked to just sit down on the benches that were along the trail and simply enjoy the moment, watching everything that they could see, like other walkers, birds, squirrels, falling leaves and… well, just anything!

Yes, walking the trail was one of their favorite things to do when they were at that park, but they also loved to go into the museum, the Reading Museum, that was also at that park.

They enjoyed looking at all the science, art, and cultural exhibits that were on display. They loved walking up and down the marble stairs, and they also loved the music that was sometimes playing in the background. But their most favorite parts of the museum were not inside the museum. They were outside the museum. They were the beautiful gardens and the foot bridges that crossed the creek. And, at least in Elne's mind, the prettiest flowers in the garden, and there were at least a gazillion of them, were the roses, the red ones, the white ones, the pink ones, the yellow ones, the orange ones, the purple ones, the... well, you get the idea, all of the roses. And, to Elne, the prettiest ones of them all were the blue ones!

You see, blue was Elne's favorite color. No one could say they knew why it was; they just knew that it was. In fact, Elne really did not even know why it was; she just knew that it was and that it always had been. So, of course, she spent most of the time that they were in the gardens, looking at and sniffing the blue roses! And sometimes, when the gardener was there, pruning the rose bushes, she even got to take one home.

Yes, they both, Elne and Area, and anyone else who was with them, when someone else was with them, loved everything that was in that park. They loved touring the museum and strolling through the gardens, walking the trail and finding the treasures, listening to the water rush over the rocks and feeding the ducks. But what they loved most of all was being together.

Now, that was no surprise to anyone who knew them, because everyone who did know them knew how important family was to them, and not just to Area and Elne, but to their whole family! That is why, to them, family was not just people who were related to each other and definitely not just people who were living together. In fact, to them, family was not just people. Nope! To them, family had a much more important meaning than that.

To them, FAMILY meant this:

Faithful Friends,

Always Aware, Anxious to Tend, Watch Over, and Care.

Merged through Blood, Adoption, or Choice,

Individuals All, but with One United Voice.

Loyal and True, Loving and Kind,

Yearning for Union by sharing One Mind!

And truth be told, they were, and are, and intend to always be a True Family!!

The End—the Loving End!

They Walked

By
Eileen DiStasio-Clark
Undated

Once upon a time, not too long ago, there was a sweet little girl, whom everyone called Elne, who loved to take walks with her just as sweet little brother, whom everyone called Jeph. They would walk across the street to their cousin's house and play with them all day. They played games like Simon Says, Hide-and-Seek, Red Light-Green Light, Hopscotch, and Red Rover. They played with Jacks and Marbles or Toy Cars and Plastic Soldiers. They played Chutes and Ladders, Candyland, and… well, a bunch of other board games. And, naturally, whether they played indoors or outdoors when they played, they always had a great day.

Now, as you probably would expect, across the street to their cousins' house was not the only place to which they walked. They would also walk to the West Reading Playground, where there was a playground, a ball field, and a pool.

Sometimes, they went to the playground to play on the Swings, the Slides, the Monkey Bars, the Jungle Gym, the Merry-Go-Round and the May Pole. And, yes, they loved doing ALL of that!

Well, wait a minute. I guess I should say that for Elne, she loved doing most of that. But when she got on the Merry-Go-Round, which she always did, by her own choice and with great enthusiasm, she got off of the Merry-Go-Round feeling quite dizzy and rather… hmmm… should I say sea-sick? I mean, she was not on the sea, but that was what she compared it to. And she did know what that felt like because every time she had ever gotten onto a boat, with hepped-up excitement, she got off the boat seasick. So much so that before she could take even two steps, she fell down and got lost in dream-land.

Now, just in case that does not make sense to you, I will say it this way. When she got off the boat, or, sometimes, before she got off the boat, she passed out! Okay, now that you understand all that, let us move on.

They also walked to the ball field, where they spent most of their time running around the track that bordered the field. But sometimes, they actually played ball on the ball field. They would play Kick Ball, kicking a soccer ball back and forth to each other. They played Baseball, sort of. One of them would toss the ball to the other one, who would do his or her best to hit the ball with the baseball bat. When the batter did hit the ball, he or she ran from base to base and then back to the home-plate, while the pitcher ran after the ball. Sometimes they played Basketball. Well, they tried to play basketball, but it was more like playing 'toss the ball' because neither one of them ever got the ball into the basket. And sometimes, they just played catch with whatever kind of ball they had with them.

Then, there were times when they would walk to the community pool, well, at least in the summer time, to go swimming, which they both really loved to do. They would swim, jump off the diving board, play Splash in the baby pool, and dive for stones. One of them would throw a stone into the pool, and the other one would dive down to retrieve it.

They also took walks on the trails by the park, and when they did, they always found things that they called treasures. Most of the time those treasures were just awesomely unusual rocks, but every once in a while, they found toys or baby bottles, books or coins, combs or socks, and things people lost and did not go back to find. Because they considered what they found to be a treasure, no matter what it was, that really made those walks a ton of fun!

They also 'took walks' up and down their stairs multiple times in a row—just to walk! But when they did that, rather than walking, they were actually running, chasing each other, and having a great time doing it.

So much did they love to walk, that they would even walk in place, which was more like marching than walking. Apparently, they thought that too, because when they did that, everyone would hear them say, "Hup, two, three, four. Hup, two, three, four," at least a dozen times, but usually more!

Now, of all the walks they took, their favorite walks were the walks they took at night around West Reading, the small, one-mile square suburb in which they lived.

Now, just in case you are wondering, I can assure you that they did not take those walks alone. Nope! On those walks, their Daddy went with them.

And the reason they took those nighttime walks was so that they could leave gifts on the doorsteps of peoples' homes without being seen! They wanted to do something nice for others without making anyone feel like they had to 'return the favor'. So, they just left the gifts at a time when they knew no one would see who was doing it.

Sometimes, they made gifts. Sometimes, they gave gifts from stuff of their own. Sometimes, with their allowance money, they bought gifts. But whatever the gift was, from wherever they got, they always left the same note with each gift, and this was that note:

"We hope you are having a wonderful life;

We know with the good, there is often strife.

But we also know that you are loved,

By family, friends, and God above!"

The End—the Pleasant End!

Bouncing Down the Steps

By
Eileen DiStasio-Clark
Undated

Once upon a time, not too long ago, there was a sweet little girl, whom everyone called Elne, who loved to bounce down the stairs with her just as sweet little sister, whom everyone called Dina. And, of course, they always had fun doing it. So...

"Wait, what did they bounce down the stairs?" you are asking.

Well, I will answer that question for you. While this may surprise you, or maybe not, what they were bouncing down the stairs was themselves.

"What?!" you are now asking, or should I say exclaiming! "How did they bounce themselves down the stairs?"

Well, I will answer that question for you, too. No, wait a minute, rather than me just answering that question for you, I will take you with me to their house. Then, you can see for yourself how they bounced themselves down the stairs. Are you okay with that? You are?! Great! Then let us be going!

"I want to go first!" Dina shouted gleefully as she and Elne scurried into their bedrooms, got their pillows off of their beds, and then ran from the bedroom to the top of the stairs.

"Okay," Elne replied, "and remember, Dina, when you get to the bottom, put your feet up so the wall hits them and not your head."

"Okay," Dina said as she sat down on her pillow on the top step, scooted slowly to the edge of the step, and then slid down the stairs.

However, despite Elne's reminder, she forgot to put her feet up. Now, so much fun was it to slide down the stairs that, even though a full body slam, with her face plastered on the wall, did not feel good, Dina was still smiling as she stepped down off the bottom step and then said to Elne, "Okay, Elne, it is your turn now."

Now, since Elne had already been sitting on her pillow at the edge of the top of the step before Dina had even gotten to the bottom of the stairs, she was ready to slide as soon as Dina stepped off the landing step, but the slide is not what she did. Instead, with her legs extended out in front of her, she bounced, literally bounced, from one step to the next, on her bottom, until she landed on the landing. And, yes, because she did have her feet up, she did not plaster herself into the wall. When she got up, she also did not step off the bottom step. Nope! She and Dina, with pillows in hand, ran back up the stairs and bounced down again and again and aga—okay, I am sure you know what they did, and they had great fun doing it.

About the time they both decided they had bounced enough, they heard Mommy calling everyone to the dinner table; it was time to eat. So, Elne and Dina ran back upstairs to put their pillows back on their beds before going to the kitchen for dinner. Well, Dina did run upstairs, but Elne walked and as she stepped on each step, she recited a line from the little "Stairs' Steps" poem she had created, and this is what that was:

On Step One…
"I love God and Jesus too.
And Holy Spirit, I also love you!
On Step Two…
I know we must repent when wrong things we do,
But just for ours, not Adam's too.
On Step Three…
I thank Jesus for what He did for us,
And I know I must live His laws without fuss.
On Step Four…
We must all have faith and repent when we wrong,
And get baptized, so the Holy Spirit can make us strong.

27

On Step Five…
God is the one who chooses who,
His works of leading and teaching will do.
On Step Six…
I know that only God could design
The plan that would help keep his children in line.
On Step Seven…
I know that God us will bless,
With many gifts, more not less.
On Step Eight…
God gave us instructions, correct and true
And learn from those is what we must do!
On Step Nine…
God reveals to us, all that He can,
But He gives it when, understand, we can
On Step Ten…
We know, one day, we will all be together,
United as one, forever and ever.
On Step Eleven…
No one can take away from anyone
The right to worship The Holy One.
On Step Twelve…
But, of course, in this life, each day
The laws of our lands we must also obey.
On Step Thirteen…
And, yes, we must always do
All that is right and good and true!
And yes! I know that know you do,
That right and good, I promise to do!
The End—the Uplifting End!

Mama's Girl, Dada's Girl, Nonna's Girl

By
Eileen DiStasio-Clark
Undated

Once upon a time, not too long ago, there was a sweet little girl whom everyone called Elne. Now, Elne was truly a 'Mama's Girl.' When she cried, and that happened daily, she wanted Mommy to hold her. When she was hungry, and that did not happen often, she wanted Mommy to give her something to eat. When she was tired, and that happened next to never (or so it seemed that way to Daddy and Mommy), she wanted Mommy to rock her. Yes, Elne was a true 'Mama's Girl.'

Elne was also a true 'Dada's Girl.' When she wanted to play horsey, which was always the case, she wanted Daddy to be her horse and give her rides on his back, all around every room in the house. When she wanted to go outside, which was just about all the time, she wanted Daddy to take her there. When she wanted to hear music, which was on a non-stop basis (or so it seemed that way to Mommy and Daddy, Area, Jeph, and Dina, and… well, you get the idea), she would grab Daddy's pant leg and 'pull' him to the piano, so he could 'make it make music' for her. Yes, Elne was truly a 'Dada's Girl.'

But Elne was also a 'Nonna's Girl.'

Wait! What?! What is a Nonna's Girl, you may be wondering. Well, I will tell you, but first let us back up for some background information that will make this make more sense.

Elne was born in the United States, in West Reading, Pennsylvania, to be exact. Mommy was born in Pennsylvania too, in Reading, and Daddy was born in Philadelphia, which is also in Pennsylvania. But… Mommy's and Daddy's mommies and daddies were not born in Philadelphia, or Reading, or West Reading. They were not born in Pennsylvania. In fact, they were not even born in the United States. Nope! Nowhere in America were they born. All of them, Daddy's daddy, Daddy's mommy, Mommy's mommy, and Mommy's daddy, were all born in Italy, a country in Europe which is all the way across the Atlantic Ocean.

Hmmm, that is kind of a silly thing to say. Of course, they were born ALL the way across the Atlantic Ocean. If they had been born only part of the way across the Atlantic Ocean, they would have been born in the Atlantic Ocean, and of course, we know that could not happen.

Well, anyway, the point is they were born in Italy and that made them Italian. And because they were Italian-born Italians, they spoke Italian. Because they spoke Italian, Grandma was really Nonna. That is the Italian word for grandmother.

So, now that you know what a Nonna is, you should also know what a 'Nonna's Girl' is, a little girl (well, she does not have to be little, but Elne sure was) who loved being with her Nonna any and every time that she could be.

Ok, so now that you know that Grandma is Nonna, you must also know what a Nonna's Girl is. And because you now know that, we will step forward again and continue.

Every time Nonna, Daddy's Mommy, who lived in the house across the street from the Staso family, came over to visit, Elne ran as fast as her tiny little legs could move her to greet her Nonna. As soon as she was in front of her, she reached her tiny little arms up as far as she could stretch them and said, with excitement, "My Nonna!" Of course, Nonna picked her up and just about always held her for almost all the time she was there to visit.

And any time Daddy or Mommy went across the street for a visit, Elne went too, and as soon as she saw Nonna, she climbed up onto her lap and gleefully exclaimed, "My Nonna!"

In fact, all the times, and for all the time, that Nonna was with them, wherever they were, Elne was with Nonna! So, yes, Elne was also a 'Nonna's Girl!'

And, truth be told, Nonna was an Elne's girl, or woman, because she loved to be with Elne just as much as Elne loved to be with her. They loved to share their adventures and new things that they had learned. They loved to read stories, sing songs, and recite poems together. They loved to listen to what everyone else was talking about, too. But of all the things they did when they were together, their favorite thing to do was make little treats for the rest of the family. Sometimes, those treats were cookies or cakes or some good treat to eat. But other times, they were little gifts, like tiny cardboard houses or penny banks made out of baby food jars, or… well, lots of different things. And on everything they made, they always attached a sweet little note. And this is what that note said:

Because God knew that we loved you and that you loved us too,

He poured down from above, His marvelous love,

So, we could be together forever!

And that is why, we will never say good-bye, not even after we die.

As long as we do good, as family,

We will be together forever!

The End—the Special End!

In Her Dreams

By
Eileen DiStasio-Clark
Undated

Once upon a time ago, what seems like a long time ago, but not really that long ago, there was a little girl, a really little girl, called Elne, who did not like taking naps! I mean, why would she?! She could barely sleep at night, so sleeping during the day was far less possible for her. In fact, it really was not possible at all. That is why naps, for her, were not naps at all. Instead of sleeping during nap time, Elne created!

"What?" you are asking. "How do you create a nap?"

Well, I guess I could answer that question like this. Elne was an amazing possum player! When she pretended to be asleep, it was very difficult to not believe she was asleep. But that is not exactly what I meant when I said instead of sleeping during nap time, Elne created. What I meant was this.

When Mommy said, "Okay, kids, it is nap time," Elne, along with her sisters and brother, who, by the way, were Area,

35

Dina, and Jeph, just ran to the living room and settled down on their favorite nap spots. Now, just so you know where those spots were, I will tell you.

Area, who found it very easy and welcoming to take a nap, always climbed onto the recliner and pushed it back as far as it would go, which was almost flat. Dina, who always curled up smaller than a tennis ball, okay, so that is a bit of an exaggeration, but she did curl up as much as she could, which was enough to make it possible for her to sleep on their big, oversized, comfy, easy chair. Jeph, who liked being wherever Elne was, would climb up onto one end of the sofa, and Elne would bounce onto the other end of the same sofa. Then, as Area, Dina, and Jeph were drifting off to sleep, Elne rolled over to face the pillows on the back of the sofa.

"If she was not possum playing, why did she do that?" you may be wondering.

Well, I will tell you why.

Their sofa had a beautiful flower pattern on it, and Elne loved to trace the flowers with her fingers. Yes, you read that right, trace the flowers with her fingers! She would start with the thumb on her right hand, trace one flower, then use her pinkie finger to trace the next flower, then her middle finger, then her ring finger, then her baby finger, with each finger tracing a different flower. Then, with her left hand, she started tracing more of the flowers with her baby finger, then her ring finger, her middle finger, then her pinkie, and then her thumb.

But since that was never enough for her to feel relaxed or content, and she did not want to wriggle and wiggle too much because she did not want to wake up Jeph, that was not all that she did. Nope! That is not the only thing. She also daydreamed.

As she laid on the sofa, pretending to nap, she would create stories in her mind, and they were pretty funny most of the time. In fact, I can share one of those stories with you.

Would you like for me to do that?

You would?!!

Okay then, I will!

After tracing all the flowers on the back pillow that she was facing, Elne, who absolutely loved horses, closed her eyes and imagined that she was riding a beautiful roan-colored Morgan Horse across an open field. It was a smooth ride, a peaceful ride, a very enjoyable ride, until...

On one side of the field, there was a pasture, and in that pasture were cows, and of course, when the cows heard the clop, clop, clop of the horses' hoofs, they began to moo, moo, moo.

Well, that startled the horse, so he began to trot faster and faster, and fas… well, you get the idea; he kept trotting faster until his trot turned into a lope, and his lope became a gallop!

Now, sweet little Elne was completely okay with that because, slow, not so slow, not so fast, or fast, she just loved to ride horses!! Well, maybe I should say she loved the horse rides her daddy and mommy would let her take when they went to the fair and special events where there were horses to ride.

Anyway, as they 'raced' across the field, she lifted herself up into jockey position and cheered the horse on. She imagined her horse jumping over the fence that surrounded the pasture where the cows were and galloping around bushes and trees, chasing the cows all over the place.

And on and on they went, until…

"Okay, kids," Mommy called, "nap time is over; you can get up!"

Since it was usually about thirty minutes, or more, before that happened Area, Jeph, and Dina were already waking up. Since Elne had never fallen asleep, she was already awake and typically responded with, "Awww, I guess I will just have to wait until tomorrow's nap to finish my ride!"

Of course, Mommy, Area, Jeph, and Dina all knew what she meant. After all, they knew how much she loved horses, and they also knew that she created the same type of daydreams every day, daydreams about horses, that she 'dreamed' while she 'napped.' And when it was time to get up from her nap, as if her daydream had been real, she would say,

Okay, horsey, now I must go.

But I will be back tomorrow, you know.

And when I am, we can run some more.

And have all the same fun that we had before.

The End—the Galloping End!

Animal Crackers

By
Eileen DiStasio-Clark
Undated

Weekend trips, well, Saturday trips to Philadelphia were a pretty common activity for the Staso family. And it made sense that they would be because at least half of Daddy's family lived there. Besides, it was not all that far away from West Reading, where the Staso family lived, so it was a pretty convenient trip to make. That was why, while their trips were not weekly, they definitely were frequent. And this had been one of the Saturdays that they had chosen to spend in Philadelphia.

They left quite early, before the kids, well Area, Jeph, and Dina, were even awake. Now, while they finished their sleep on the back seat in the car, Elne, who was out of bed even before Daddy and Mommy got up, sat in the middle of the front seat, squirming and squiggling all the way to Uncle Omas' and Aunt Rasha's house.

Now, they were pretty early risers too, so it was no surprise that they were already up and were in the process of preparing breakfast. Since the Stasos had not eaten before they left, Aunt Rasha cooked enough breakfast, which was scrambled eggs, bacon and toast, for everyone. Well, everyone except Elne. Because they all knew how much Elne hated food, especially things like eggs and bacon or anything that came from an animal, Aunt Rasha made a bowl of oatmeal for her. Then, after they all cleaned up the breakfast dishes and put away the left-over food, they went to the living room.

Daddy, Mommy, Uncle Omas, and Aunt Rasha sat on the couches and talked and talked about this, that, everything else, and nothing at all. While they did that, the kids sat on the floor playing Pick-Up-Sticks and Marbles.

After their visit with Uncle Omas and Aunt Rasha, they went to Uncle Raner's house where the kids played with their cousins while the parents sat and talked, and talked, and tal… well, you know what they did.

Then, they met up with their Uncle Lar and his kids at a luncheonette, where they all enjoyed lunch together before going to the City Street Market. After they were all done shopping for everything they really did not need, the Stasos said bye-bye to their cousins, or nephews and nieces, and their uncle or brother-in-law, who then headed home.

The Staso family then went to visit the sites they visited almost every time they were in Philadelphia. They toured Independence Hall, saw the Liberty Bell, walked through the Betsy Ross house, and the Ben Franklin Museum. They visited Carpenter's Hall and took a walk on the path next to the Schuylkill River. Finally, they went to ride the trolley. Now, because that was so much fun, and because they all loved that so much, they took, not just one ride but… hmmm… I do not know how many trolley rides they took, but I do know that it was quite a few! Enough so that by the time they got off the trolley the last time that they had gotten on it, it was time to go home.

Now, while Daddy and Mommy walked to the car, Jeph, Area, Dina, and Elne—the kids—ran to the car. When Daddy and Mommy caught up with them and Daddy unlocked the doors, the kids jumped into the car and seated themselves onto their favorite seats. Jeph sat on the back seat by the driver's side window. Area sat on the back seat by the passenger's side window. Dina sat on the front seat between Daddy and Mommy. And Elne sat in the back but not on the seat; she sat on the hump in the middle of the floor so as to be able to use the seat as a desk.

Quick Side Note: In case you are wondering why they were not buckled on the seat with the seat belts, I will explain that to you. These kids were little kids a long time ago before cars even had seat belts. So, there was no way they could be buckled into the seats with seat belts.

Now that you understand that let us go back to the other side.

As Daddy pulled away from the curb, Elne put her drawing pad on the seat, pulled a pencil out of her pocket, and began to draw. She drew the Liberty Bell, in as much detail as she could. Then she drew the Schuylkill River, emphasizing its ebb and flow with every bump of the car, and was almost done when…

"No!" Jeph screamed, "Stop, Daddy! Stop!"

So startling was Jeph's scream that Area bounced off her seat; Elne, with her pencil, poked a hole in the seat; Mommy and Dina swiftly turned their heads and looked over the front seatback, and Daddy, calmly said, "What is wrong, Jeph?"

Jeph, had been kneeling on the seat, facing the door, with his arms on the door where the window rolled down into it, and his head was sticking out of the window. He always did that when the weather permitted it because he loved the feel of the wind! He was also holding a little box of Animal Crackers, which was tapping against the door, as the wind blew it wildly!

So, when Daddy drove over the trolly tracks, which bounced the car like a basketball on the court during a hepped-up game, Jeph, who bounced up and down with the car, lost hold of his Animal Crackers. As he leaned even farther out of the window, 'reaching for them,' he screamed for Daddy to stop so he could rescue the 'animals' from the trolley that they all knew because they came very regularly, would be coming soon.

Daddy, being the loving person that he was, made a U-Turn at the next intersection, where there was no other traffic present, drove back to the intersection where the trolley tracks were, and parked alongside the curb of the sidewalk. He got out, and so did Jeph, took Jeph's hand, so he could keep him by his side, and walked cautiously to the tracks.

It took less than a moment to find the Animal Crackers, well, to find the squashed box that the Animal Crackers had been in. Apparently, a car had run over them.

Poor Jeph, he was so sad. After picking up the box, they walked back to the car, got in and then…

Daddy, being the sweet Daddy that he was, drove to the nearest grocery store, where they got another box, well boxes, of Animal Crackers before heading home.

Oh, and on the rest of the trip back to West Reading, Jeph kept his box of Animal Crackers safely inside the car!

The End—the Smart End!

We Can Start With a Cheer!

By
Eileen DiStasio-Clark
Undated

Out the front door of their Row Home, she hurried across their front porch and down the steps she hustled. Up the hill she ran, all four and a half blocks, then turning to the right, she scuttled another two blocks before turning left, racing the coming cars as she crossed each street. Then, up the steps and through the front doors of the school building, she bustled. Up some more stairs, she hopped, skipping over every other step, and then, into her classroom, she bounded, plopping herself, with no grace at all, onto her seat at her desk.

Then, looking around in great astonishment, she wondered, 'Where is everyone?!'

Thinking she was late for school because she did leave the house a bit later than she usually did, she expected to be the last one in the room. Instead, she was the first one in the room. In fact, she was the only one in the room because not even her teacher was there. And that was definitely odd because her teacher was always there before any of the students were.

"This is weird," she said aloud, "where is everyone? I guess I really am the first one here."

For a little while, she just sat quietly, wondering what was going on, or what had happened, or wh… well, I am pretty sure that you have a pretty good idea what she was thinking. But just in case I am wrong, and you do not have a pretty good idea of what she was thinking, I will tell you. She was wondering where everyone was. She did not know what to think because she could not come up with any answers to that question. So, she just sat there.

Now, of course, she was not just sitting there, and she was not sitting still, and she was not doing nothing, because she was not someone who was okay, or even able, to sit still and do nothing. Nope! Doing nothing was not her style.

So, first, she pulled her Spelling book out of her desk and wrote and rewrote all of the words that were a part of that week's lesson. Then, when she was done with that, and there was still no one else in the room, she put her Spelling book back on her desk and pulled out her Math book. She went over all the problems in the chapter that they had begun the day before, as well as reviewing her homework assignment.

When she was done with that, and after she put her Math book back in her desk, she reached for her Literature book, with the intent to read the next story, but just as she was about to pull it out of her desk, after what seemed to her to be an eternity of time, Mrs. Loton, her homeroom and English teacher, walked into the room and, with startled expression said, "Oh my goodness, Elne! Why are you sitting there? Everyone has been waiting for you for… well however long we have been waiting, we have been waiting for you!"

"Waiting for me?" the confused Elne asked, "Why are— Whoever is waiting for me, waiting for me, and where are they waiting?"

"Your class is waiting for you," her teacher replied, "in the gym! We all have all been in the gym, waiting for you for quite some time."

"Why are they in the gym?" Elne asked, totally confused. "And why are you all waiting for me? You do not need to wait for anyone to get here before you start your classes."

"Do you not remember?" Mrs. Loton asked with obvious astonishment. Then explained, "You and your cheerleading team were given the assignment to perform for us this morning. Remember, Elne, since you are the leader of your cheerleading squad, I asked you to prepare a cheer that we could use as an introduction to the lesson I prepared on Loyalty?"

"Oh, my goodness!!" Elne replied with hyped-up energy. "I totally forgot!!" Then, after reaching into her book-bag and pulling out several other sheets of paper while saying no more, and without waiting for her teacher, she jumped up from her seat, dashed out of the room, ran down the hall to the stairway, and scampered to the gym.

Elne called for her Cheerleading Squad to gather at the end of the bleachers and asked the rest of her classmates to seat themselves on the bleachers. Then, as Mrs. Loton entered the gym, Elne gave her the papers that she had pulled out of her bookbag and asked her to group the kids into four groups and give them each one of the sheets. She explained that those groups, in the order in which their sheets were numbered, would repeat what was on the papers each time the squad paused their cheering.

While Mrs. Loton grouped the kids on the bleachers and gave them their papers to review, Elne reviewed with the

Cheerleading Squad the cheer that she had written for them to deliver.

Then, after they all had enough time to ready themselves, with the Cheerleading Squad having reviewed the cheer and their classmates seated in their groups on the bleachers, they began their cheer, and this is how that went.

Cheerleading Squad
Rah, rah, here we go!
Group One
What is it you want us to know?
Cheerleading Squad
With the West Reading Cowboys,
we stand tall!
Group Two
Well, we cheer with you, one and all.
Cheerleading Squad
Good! Great! Then all stand up.
Group Three
So, we can carry the Loyalty cup!
Cheerleading Squad
Loyalty! Loyalty! Full and True!!
Group Four
That is what we all feel for you!
And the cheers continued!!

The End—the Cheerful End!

The Family's Funniest Fable

By
Eileen DiStasio-Clark
Undated

The fire was blazing! And it was beautiful! It was the hottest, biggest, most roaring campfire they had ever had and, since they loved camping so much, they had had many!!!! So, after a full day of playing games, Ring Toss, Horseshoes, Catch-Me-If-You-Can, Happy-Hunting, taking hikes, wading in the creek, and climbing trees, they were all sitting around the campfire, roasting marshmallows, singing happy songs, reciting poems, and recounting their daily adventures. Then it was time for their Tale-Tellings, and everyone was ready for that! I mean, why would they not be? That was there most favorite part of sitting around the campfires, and they all took turns, with a different person beginning the Tale-Telling each night. Now, just so you know, this is how they determined who would be the first one to tell that night's tale.

Everyone searched all over the camp site until they each had found a nice-sized stone. Then, they walked down the little hill that led to the path that was next to the creek and lined up in the order in which they were going to toss their stones. Whoever tossed their stone the farthest would be the one to tell the tale. Well, actually, they were just the first ones to tell the tale because, as I said, they always took turns so that everyone could be a Tale-Teller.

Now, starting with the youngest and proceeding to the oldest, this is how the stone-throwing went.

First, Dina, who was quite young, threw her stone, or should I say, dropped her stone. It landed just in front of her feet!

Next, Jeph threw his stone. It crossed the path on which they were standing, the narrow path, but went no farther than that!

Next, Elne threw her stone. It went to the edge of the creek, close enough to the water to get wet but not close enough to go in.

Next, Area threw her stone. It did go into the creek, about as far in from the bank as she was up, that is tall, from the ground.

Then it was Mommy's turn. Her toss was great! The stone landed in the middle of the creek.

Finally, it was Daddy's turn. His toss was awesome! It landed on the bank on the other side of the creek. So, he was the one who would tell the first silly tale that night!

Now, before that adventure began, they were confronted with another one. You see, on their way back to the campsite, they saw a raccoon sitting on their table with his nose stuck into one of their food bags. Well, without discussion, they all decided that that was not okay. Therefore, they all picked up a pinecone and began running toward the table. When they got close enough to do so, they threw their pinecones at the raccoon. Naturally, the raccoon jumped off the table and scampered into the woods, but not before standing up and hissing at them, which made them all laugh. I mean really, it sounded so cute!

Then, after cleaning up the mess that the raccoon had made and securing everything in their coolers and baskets, they went back to the fire pit, where the fire was still glowing, sat down in their camping chairs, and listened intently as Daddy began relating what, after he was done sharing it, they all identified as the Family's Funniest Fable, which, by the way, even though they called it a fable, it really was a true story!

Now, you are probably wondering what that tale was, so I will tell you.

"Well," Daddy began, "we all know how much Elne loves animals! In fact, she loves them so much that she really does not display too much sense when animals are around, any kind of animal!"

Heads nodded, with everyone smiling and even beginning to giggle, and that included Elne.

Daddy continued, "She was the 'grand-old-age' of four and had just gotten out of bed. After saying her morning prayers, and without bothering to change out of her pajamas, she hopped, skipped, and jumped through the bedrooms and down the steps, but when she got to the landing step, she stopped!"

Okay, so now the giggles had grown into 'quiet' laughter. Even Daddy was beginning to chuckle a little, but he managed to keep charge of himself and continue, "Quietly, she stepped onto the bottom step and to the floor, then got down on her knees, leaned forward, and began petting the rat that had somehow gotten into the house."

"I will never understand," Mommy said between her chuckles, "why you thought it was okay to pet a rat!"

"He was so cute!" Elne said, with a tone of true innocence in her voice.

"But," Daddy interjected, "when Mommy, as she was coming down the stairs, saw what Elne was doing, screamed with very vocalized alarm for Elne to get away from that. Of course that scared the rat, who ran under the radiator in the kitchen, and it also scared Elne, who screamed back, ran across the living room, and hid under the piano bench."

"Well," Elne interjected, "I thought I was in trouble, so I was scared too."

"Yeah," Jeph added, "but not enough because then, instead of going to Mommy for a comforting hug, you went to the kitchen to get the rat, but when you could not find him, you sat down and cried."

"Well," Elne explained, "I just wanted him to be okay, and when I could not find him, I did not know what to think, or say, or do, but I had to do something, so I cried. And besides, I was sad; he would have been a sweet little pet."

"And now you see," Daddy said, as he finished the tale, "why that tale is one of our craziest tales!"

Well, needless to say, but I will say it anyway, the laughing simply heightened all the more and did not stop for a long time. But then, neither did the Family's Funniest Fables, and that was okay because that way, everyone could turn in for the night with joy in their hearts and happiness in their mind.

The End—the Joyful End!

Lefty, Come Back Here!

By
Eileen DiStasio-Clark
Undated

It was a nice warm day, early in the summer, probably the first or maybe the second week in June. The sun was rising, welcoming the day with its bright shining rays. The air was lightly breezy, sweeping the earth with the comforting scents it blew up from the gardens. The birds were singing, greeting everyone with their peaceful, good morning songs. And Lefty, the cute little beagle who was the Staso family pet, was barking, letting everyone, the whole neighborhood, know that he was ready for his morning walk.

Now, while most of the Staso family were still asleep, or at least still in bed, if they were awake, Elne was not! Nope! Since sleep was not one of her greatest talents, actually, it was not one of her talents at all, she was already awake and out of bed. In fact, she was already ready for the day. She had said her prayers, made her bed, got dressed, and was on her way downstairs when

Lefty began his barking. Come to think of it, he probably heard her coming down the stairs and was barking, "Good morning."

So, once off the bottom step, Elne scooted through the dining room, to the kitchen, got Lefty's leash off the hook in the coat closet, clipped it to his collar, and then, quietly, opened the kitchen door, walked Lefty outside, to the back of the back yard, went through the gate to the field that was across the alley, which was really Grape Street, and then walked a small bit of a way onto the field next to the alley.

There, she stopped long enough for him to take care of his morning business. When he was done, they walked across the rest of the field up to 3rd Avenue, made a left turn, and headed for the playground, which was only about 7 or 8 blocks. However, though not to her surprise, their walk that morning was actually quite a bit longer than that. And no, it was not because she took detours and made route changes, which she often did because she really loves to take walks. Nope! Not at all!

That day, it was Lefty who had a different idea than Elne had of what their walk should be. And, truth be told, most of the time, their walks were patterned after his idea, even though she tried the best she could to pattern them after her idea. Now, on that day, her idea was to walk to the playground, run, with Lefty, around the track 4 times, which would be her daily mile run, and then go back home. But Lefty's idea! Well, just read on and you will get the idea!

They walked quietly, but with a pepped-up step. Neither of them seemed to know any other way to walk. Anyway, they walked about three blocks, crossing Chestnut Street, Kline Street, and Spruce Street. Well, they started to cross Spruce Street in a quiet manner, but when Lefty saw a squirrel . . . Well, let me just say this; it was not a quiet walk anymore.

Lefty dashed after the squirrel, with such unexpected force that it pulled Elne off balance. She tried to recapture her balance, but to no avail. She fell to the ground, right in the middle of the intersection, and when she did, she lost hold of the leash. As quickly as she could, she jumped up off the street and began chasing Lefty.

He ran up Spruce Street to 4th Avenue; Elne did too, screaming all the way, "Lefty, come back here!" Did he stop? Did he go back to her? Nope, he just kept running.

He ran down 4th Avenue to Pine Street and then up Pine Street to Ann Street; Elne did too, screaming even louder,

"Lefty, come back here!" Did he stop there? Nope, he just kept running, even faster.

He ran down Ann Street to Sunset Road, and then onto Sycamore Road; Elne did too, screaming and screaming, "Lefty, come back here!" Did he stop then? Yes, he actually did stop. In fact, he even turned around, wagging his tail with all the force of a hurricane wind. Well, maybe not that much, but quite a lot for a little, almost baby sized, beagle. Anyway, he wagged and wagged, and wa. . . well, you know what he did, he wagged his tail until Elne was just in front of him, putting out her hand to pick up the leash. As she was just about to grab it, he ran off again!

Of course, Elne did too, running after him, screaming all the way to the playground, which is where she wanted to go anyway, "Lefty, come back here!"

Well, needless to say, but I will say it anyway, he did not do what she said. In fact, she had to chase him around the track six times before he changed his route. Then, she had to chase him back and forth and forth and back, again and again, across and around the ball field. Hmmm, I think we should just move on. As a matter of fact, that is what we have to do to keep up with them because they just kept running.

He ran, and she chased him, off the playground, down, or was it up, Playground Drive to Parkview Road, and back to 3rd Avenue, where, again, he stopped, turned to Elne, all the while wagging his tail, with a 'doggie grin' on his face. And, yes, when she stopped and reached out to pick up his leash, he took off again!

Down 3rd Avenue to Chestnut Street, Lefty ran and Elne chased, this time calling, not screaming, "Lefty, come back here." But to no avail; he just kept running. So, once at the corner of Chestnut Street, Elne decided to try a different tactic. Instead of chasing Lefty, she called out to him, "Lefty, I am going home." Then, as she started down the hill to her house, which was just 6 houses from the corner, Lefty, who was about 6 houses up the street on the other side of 3rd Avenue, stopped, turned toward Elne, and watched.

As Elne walked down the block to her house, Lefty began to follow her. As Elne walked up the steps to their front porch, Lefty stopped at the bottom step and looked up at her. When she turned to look at him, he took a few steps back, but then...

When Elne opened the front door to go into the house, she turned to Lefty and said one more time, "Lefty, come." And that time he did. He ran up the steps, across the porch, into the house, and sat on the living room rug, looking at Elne with that 'doggie grin' on his face.

Interestingly, as Elne took the leash off Lefty's collar and put it away, then got his breakfast for him, she thought, 'Wow! It seems to me that the gentle approach, God's approach, is not only the best approach for people, but for animals too! I will have to remember that, always!"

The End—the Gentle End!

Out Of Gas

By
Eileen DiStasio-Clark
1986

"Why didn't you get any gas, Mommy?" asked Prisca, as we squeezed between the cars crowding the gas pumps.

"Because they only have unleaded gas," Mommy explained, "and Daddy said we should always use regular gas in Cranky."

Side Note: Just in case you are wondering, Cranky was what the Gib family called their van because it always had one kind of problem or another. At least that is what it seemed like to a them—all of them. Now, back to the other side.

"Why didn't we get gas here?" Marah asked, as they left the second gas station Mommy had pulled into.

"Because here you have to pay for the gas before you pump it and I do not know how much it will cost," Mommy replied. "I want to fill up the tank so we do not run out of gas and get stuck somewhere."

Now, it was not the best of days to be riding around in a temperamental, 'open-window-air-cooled' van, as the temperatures were already in the nineties, and Jacksonville's Phillips Highway, at least the part they were on, is not exactly overcrowded with home or businesses. But it was necessary, because they needed supplies for the Ward Pageant, for which preparation time was not standing still, and the only store that had what they needed was on the Phillips Highway.

Now, they were just a few miles down the road from the second gas station Mommy had pulled into and out of, when Cranky began sputtering. "Uh-oh!" Mommy exclaimed softly.

"What's the matter?" Marah asked, as Cranky's sputtering turned into 'hiccups' and 'coughs'.

"I think Cranky is running out of gas," Mommy replied calmly.

Unfortunately, she was right. As they drifted to a dead stop on the grassy shoulder of the highway, silence momentarily replaced the childhood chatter, which usually permeated the van. In seconds, however, that silence was shattered by fearful cries from all the occupants on the seats in the back of the van.

"I want to go home!" cried Joanna.

"Let's go back to that gas station!" cried Prisca.

66

"We cannot," explained Mommy, as she unbuckled her seat-belt and turned to the children. "Cranky will not go anywhere without gas. That is why we are here now."

That was when Luke joined the Crying Choir Even though he really did not know why he was crying. He figured, if his sisters were crying, there must be a good reason to cry, so he did!

Abbie just sat quietly. She seemed bewildered by the whole situation. But, before long, she joined the Crying Choir too.

Marah just gave Mommy one of those, 'Oh, Mommy' looks and asked, "What are we going to do?"

"We are not going to do anything," Mommy answered.

"I want to go home!" rang out the Crying Choir.

Now, with a van-load of children, and no stroller for the baby, they could not walk anywhere. So, Mommy explained to them, "It would not be safe for us to leave the van. And, cars do not have telephones so we cannot call anyone. So, we will have to sit here and wait for someone to stop to help us. There is nothing else we can do."

"I want Daddy to help us!" the crying choir bellowed.

"So do I," Mommy echoed. Then, in an attempt to lighten the 'crisis', Mommie added, "What do you think Daddy will say?"

"I don't know," they responded in unison.

"I do," Mommy replied. "He will give me one of those, 'I can't believe you did that' looks." Then, speaking in her best 'Daddy imitation voice,' added, "And he will say to me, 'I told you to get gas. Why didn't you get it on your way home this morning, after you dropped me off at work. What am I going to do with you?!'"

Now, that did get a little chuckle our of the kids, but there was still much apprehension. And that was what inspired Marah to ask, "What if no one stops?"

"Someone will help us," Mommy assured her. "Heavenly Father will see to that. He will help us because He knows that right now, we cannot help ourselves."

"Could we say a prayer?" Prisca asked.

"That is an excellent idea!" Mommy replied.

"Can we all say one?" Joanna asked.

"We sure can," Mommy stated firmly, and with great appreciation for her children's readiness to turn to Heavenly Father and pray.

For sever moments there was silence again. But that time it was a reverent silence, as they all—Mommy, Marah, Prisca, Joanna, Luke, and Abbie—folded their arms, bowed their heads, and put in their pleas for heavenly help. Oh! And Joanna said two prayers, one for herself and one for Baba, who was just a baby.

After a round of seven Amens, Mommy petitioned a piece of cloth from Abbie. Abbie reached into the bag that was on the floor and pulled out a small piece of material that Mommy had got at the store to use to make a quilt. She tossed it over then front seat back to Mommy, who tied it to the sideview mirror, and then turned on the flashers. As she watched the different 'people types' go by, she offered one more silent prayer, "Please, Heavenly Father, let it be someone good who stops."

Four cars and a trailer later, a white truck slowed to a stop, on the grassy shoulder, behind them. After a moment, a pleasant looking man, perhaps in his fifties, got out of the truck and walked up to the driver's door. Through the window, he handed her a small white card with this explanation, "This is my business card, so you'll know I want to help you and not hurt you. I saw all the kids and figured you probably needed help."

With a sigh of relief, Mommy whispered a thank you to Heavenly Father, then said to the man, "I think we are just out of gas. I knew I needed some, and that is what it felt like when the van stopped."

"Just out of gas?" he questioned. "Are you sure?

"Yes, I am pretty sure," Mommy replied.

"OK," he said, "I'll go get some gas and see if we can get you going again."

As he pulled back onto the highway, Prisca remarked, "Heavenly Father sure works fast."

Now, to that, everyone smiled.

It was less than fifteen minutes later, and when Mommy was in the middle of changing Baba's diaper, that the man returned, emptied the gas into Cranky's tank, and suggested, "Give it a try now and see what happens."

He waited patiently through Cranky's usual stubborn turn over, one more diaper change, the customary 'five-minute' buckle-up of all the kids, and Mommy's cautious re-entry into traffic, before pulling away himself. Though they all had said their thankyous to him, it seemed they needed to do something more to show their gratitude. After all, not only did he stop to help them, but he would not even let Mommy pay for the gas.

As Mommy listened to the kids' comments, which included, "He sure was a nice man," "That was really nice of him," "I think he is an angel," she felt a comforting warmth! It seemed to her that, scary as this experience was at first, it turned out to be a good experience because of what the kids seem to have learned.

She also listened to their questions, which included, "Do you think he goes to our church?" And from that, she knew exactly what they should do. A personalized Book of Mormon would quickly be on its way to Charles L. Altendorf.

So, the first thing they did when they got home—well, okay, not the first thing. The first they did after they got into the house, was look through all the stuff they had bought and put it away. Then they got a snack to eat for breakfast, after which they started school. So, it was really the first thing they did after school was over. And what they did when school was over was get a Book of Mormon off the shelf where they kept all their scriptures, wrote a special thank you note in the front of the book, wrapped in up in mailing paper, and took it to the Post Office.

When they got back home, Daddy was already there and wanted to know where they had been. So, as you would probably expect, they all joined in relating the tale of the day to Daddy, after which he looked at Mommy, with one of 'those looks' and said, "I told you to get gas! Why didn't you get it on your way home this morning? What am I going to do with you."

And, of course, that made everyone laugh, including Mommy!

The End—the Sweet End!

Johnny, Go to Sleep

By
Eileen DiStasio-Clark
Autumn 2009

Adapted from a childhood bedtime story which was adapted from an old folktale.

Johnny was a rambunctious little guy. He bounced off the walls, bounded up and down the stairs, and whirled through the house all day long! One would have thought that Johnny would be worn out by the time his mommy said, "OK, Johnny, it is time for bed." But not Johnny; Johnny never wanted to go to bed.

"I'm not tired," Johnny whined.

"Yes, you are," Mommy assured him, as she directed him toward the steps. "It is time to take your bath and go to bed... upstairs... now."

Johnny gave his daddy a kiss goodnight, then obediently, but reluctantly, started toward the stairs. As he passed the kitchen, he *realized* he was thirsty. "I need water," he said, turning toward the kitchen.

"You can get it in the bathroom," Mommy said, taking his hand, and turning him back to the stairs. "...to the bathroom, now."

Nearing the stairs, Johnny suddenly *remembered*, "I forgot my Lego man," he cried, turning back to the living room.

"It is right here," Mommy said, taking it out of her pocket and turning him back to the stairs as she slipped it into his hand.

So, obediently but reluctantly, Johnny sulked his way to the stairs. Now, like all little boys, Johnny did not know how to walk up steps. Instead, he jumped onto the first step and began to tap-dance. "One, two, take off my shoes," he said as he sat down on the second step to do just that.

Keeping the rhythm going, as she picked up his shoes, Mommy said, "Three, four, no stalling anymore."

"Five, six, watch my tricks," Johnny continued, as he hopped and tapped, and jumped and spun up the next three or four steps.

From the top of the stairs Mommy called, "Seven, eight, don't make me wait," then she turned down the hallway to the bathroom.

75

Jumping onto the top step, Johnny sang, "Nine, ten, let's do it again."

But before he could turn around, he heard Mommy say, in her very *"Mommy"* kind of voice, "Don't you dare! Get in here, now!"

Obediently but reluctantly, Johnny got into the bath. Now usually, during the day, it takes Johnny a grand total of a couple dozen minutes to do the things he does, but when it comes to his bath…

With the dishes done, the counters wiped clean, the laundry folded and the dog put out in his kennel for the night, Mommy went to say goodnight to Johnny, but he was not in his bed.

"Johnny," Mommy said, peeking into the bathroom, "out of the tub; you look like a prune!"

"But, Mommy…" Johnny began.

"Now, Johnny!" Mommy said in her very *"Mommy"* kind of voice. So, out he got.

Nevertheless, if his bath was not long enough, his teeth brushing was. "What is taking you so long?" Mommy asked, as she put the last of the linens in the closet.

"I have a lot of teeth," Johnny replied.

"Not that many, Johnny," Mommy retorted.

"But you said three minutes," Johnny reminded her.

"You are only supposed to take two or three minutes to brush all your teeth, Johnny," she clarified, "not each tooth. Speed it up!"

Finally, after a dozen more complaints about "missing all the fun," six or seven offers to "keep Daddy and Mommy company," several glasses of water, and two or three trips to the bathroom, Johnny went obediently but reluctantly, and unhappily, to his room. He knelt down with his mommy to say his prayers and blessed everyone... in the world... individually... twice—or so it seemed to Mommy, whose knees were not quite as tough as Johnny's were.

After he had said his prayers, Johnny kissed his mommy goodnight, slid between his sheets, laid his head down, closed his eyes, but did not go to sleep. In fact, his mommy was not even down all the stairs when she heard, "Mommy, I did not give you a kiss."

"Yes, you did," Mommy assured him. "Good-night, Johnny."

She was just turning down the hall when she heard, "Mommy, I did not give Daddy a kiss."

"Yes, you did," Mommy assured him. "Good-night, Johnny."

As she settled down onto the sofa next to Daddy, she heard, "Mommy, I'm hungry."

"No, you are not," Mommy said. "You ate enough dinner to feed the neighborhood. Now, go to sleep!"

"Mommy, I'm thirsty," Johnny called.

"No, you are not," Mommy said. "You drank enough water to fill a fish tank. Go to sleep!"

"Mommy, I'm scared," Johnny called again.

"Johnny," Mommy called back, with a hint of impatience in her very *"Mommy"* kind of voice. "You are not scared! Nothing scares you. In fact, Godzilla runs away when he sees you coming! Now… go… to… sleep!"

Johnny had run out of reasons to get out of bed. So, he closed his eyes and laid there quietly for a little while – a very little while. Then, "Moooommyyyy…"

But this time Daddy answered. "Johnny, if you do not go to sleep, NOW, the Sandy Man might come up there and take you away to Slumber Land."

That got Johnny quiet—for a while, for as long as he could stand it, but then…

"Mommy…" Mommy did not answer.

"Daddy…" Daddy did not answer.

"Mommy…" silence answered.

Johnny got out of bed. He tiptoed quietly across the room. He slowly turned the knob of his bedroom door.

Just as he was about to pull the door open, he heard a sort of quiet, kind of amusingly spooky voice say, "Johnny, I'm on the first step."

Johnny stood stone still, listening, but silence was all he heard.

He began again to open the door, but again he heard a sort of quiet, kind of amusingly spooky voice say, "Johnny, I'm on the second step."

Again, Johnny stood stone still and listened. Again, all Johnny heard was silence.

But this time, before he could even think about opening the door, he heard that sort of quiet, kind of amusingly spooky voice say, "Johnny, I'm on the third step, and I'm coming to get you."

Johnny ran across the room as the sort of quiet, kind of amusingly spooky voice was saying, "Johnny, I'm on the fourth step."

In one huge kangaroo jump, he bounced onto his bed and under his covers.

"Johnny, I'm on the fifth step."

"Who are you?" Johnny asked from under the covers.

"Johnny, I'm Sandy Man, and I'm on the sixth step."

"What do you want?" Johnny demanded to know from under his pillow.

"Johnny, I'm on the seventh step and want to take you to Slumber Land."

"Go away!" Johnny yelled.

"Johnny, I'm on the eighth step."

"Mo—," Johnny was just about to call for his mommy when he remembered that Daddy had said the Sandy Man would only come if he did not go to sleep.

"Maybe," he whispered to himself, "if I pretend I am sleeping, he will go away." So, Johnny said, "Don't bother me; I'm sleeping." And he snored, "Honk-pish-pish-pooh."

"Johnny, I'm on the ninth…"

Johnny snored louder, "Honk-Pish-Pish-Pooh."

"Johnny, I'm…"

He snored even louder, "HONK-PISH-PISH-POOH!"

Then the sort of quiet, kind of amusingly spooky voice chanted, "Honk-pish-pish-pooh, simply will not do; I have come for you; Honk-pish-pish-pooh."

Johnny was quiet and still.

"Johnny, I'm in your room; are you awake?"

But Johnny did not answer.

"Johnny, I'm beside your bed; are you awake?"

Johnny still did not answer. In fact, there was no sound or movement at all from Johnny's bed.

The Sandy Man leaned over Johnny to see if he was awake. But he was not. Johnny had fallen fast asleep; actually, Johnny had fallen asleep, fast.

So, the Sandy Man turned around and left the room. Outside the door, Mommy waited. "Is he asleep?" she tiredly asked.

"You bet!" replied Daddy. "It works every time."

As Mommy and Daddy headed down the hallway to their room, Johnny smiled sleepily, yawning his way into Slumber Land, and whispered, "Good night, Sandy, Daddy, and Mommy," and then slept peacefully all night long.

The End—the Sleepy End!

A Conversation In the Cemetery

By

Eileen DiStasio-Clark

October, 2024

Whenever the Staso family went to Philadelphia to visit their relatives, they also stopped at the cemetery to visit their relatives. At least, that is what Elne believed they were doing. And why not? Even though a cemetery is where we retire people when it is their time to move on from this world, it is still possible for them to visit us when Heavenly Father okays that and to help us when we need help. So, to Elne, there was no better place to talk to them than at the cemetery where they 'were'. And there was one day, in particular, that Elne really needed to talk to her Staso grandparents. So, when they went to the cemetery, Elne sat down by the 'big stone tablets' as she called them, the tombstones, and this is what happened.

"Nonno Rendaw, are you here?" Elne whispered quietly.

"Nonna Shartee, are you here?" she added.

"Nonno, Nonna," she whispered again, "I want to ask you a question. Are you here?"

Side Note: Just in case I forgot to tell you before, I will tell you now. The Staso family was 100 percent Italian. In fact, on both sides of the family, mommy's and daddy's, all four of their grandparents had come to America from Italy. So, since Italian was spoken a lot when the families got together, Nonno, which is grandfather in Italian, and Nonna, which is grandmother in Italian, were what grandpa and grandma were called. That makes sense. Right? Right! So now that you understand that, let us get back to the other side.

Being a rather peaceful child, Elne did not have a hard time—well, not too hard of a time—waiting for a reply. But because she was also not one to sit and do nothing, she began to sing.

And this is what she sang:

I love my Nonno; I do; I do.
I love my Nonno; it is true; it is true.
I love him; I love him; I love him; I do.
I love my Nonno; I really, really, really, really do!

And when she was done singing that, she sang this:

I love my Nonna; I do; I do.
I love my Nonna; it is true; it is true.

83

I love her; I love her; I love her; I do.

I love my Nonna; I really, really, really, really do!

And when she was done singing that, well, even a little before she was actually done singing, she began to feel a feeling that she had not felt before, well, at least not for some time. It was a peaceful feeling, a gentle and quiet feeling; it was a warm feeling. And, as she was feeling that feeling, she also noticed that, even though it had been bright because it was a sunny day, there seemed to be an even brighter brightness gathering around her. Then, when she looked up in the direction of the light, she saw them!

"Nonno! Nonna!" Elne exclaimed as she stood up, all the while looking up at the two… should I say persons, or should I say angels?

Well, however you would identify them, I know you know who I mean. Standing above the ground, clothed in white robes and with a halo of shining light surrounding them, were Nonno Rendaw and Nonna Shartee.

As Elne stood stone still, in complete silence, and looked at them with awe, together, they spoke to her with gentle, quiet, sweet words, saying, "Elne, yes! We love you! We love all of you, your Daddy, your Mommy, your sisters and your brother. We love all of our families!"

84

"And, yes, Elne," Nonno added, "we are waiting for you! We are doing all that we need to do here and ask you to do all that you need to do there so that we can be together forever."

"Oh, my goodness!" Elne replied after a little bit longer than a short moment of awe. When she was finally able to speak again, she said, "I want all our families to be together forever too. I knew that having Heavenly Father's true gospel makes that possible for those who want it and do what it takes to have it, but I did not know if I really knew what you thought. That is why I was wondering if, when I am able to, you would like me to do then Temple Work for you. Do you know what I mean?"

"Yes," Nonna answered, "we do, and yes, we do want you and your parents to do that for us. We have been waiting patiently."

Then, again both together, as they departed, they said, "Elne, we love you. Continue to be good. Be better. Be your best!"

Elne sat back down on the ground by the 'Stone Tablets', looked at them with a loving expression, and then, again, sang:

I love my Nonno; I do; I do.
I love my Nonno; it is true; it is true.
I love him; I love him; I love him; I do.
I love my Nonno; I really, really, really, really do!

I love my Nonna; I do; I do.

I love my Nonna; it is true; it is true.

I love her; I love her; I love her; I do.

I love my Nonna; I really, really, really, really do!

The End—the Eternal End!

Poems from My Daddy and Me
Prayer Is the Answer

By

Joseph DeStasio Sr.

Undated

Some people dread life's ending;
They live in constant fear,
Although they seldom ever know,
If death is far or near.

This fright stems from the lack of faith
In what will come to be,
When it is time to say goodbye,
For all Eternity.

The Souls aglow with faith and hope,
Have little time to doubt.
They believe in the Hereafter,
And so; they are devout!

This is the miracle of faith,
Gained by the use of power,
That serves to make us happy,
And helps us to prepare.

If those who dread life's ending,
Would only pause to pray,
The doubts and fears they entertain,
Would swiftly drift away.

And so it is, each one of us,
Should turn our thoughts to praying.
It's not the leaving that is hard;
The toughest part is staying.

Andrina

By

Joseph DeStasio Sr.

Undated

Words cannot express,
This wonderful day.
Words cannot explain,
Why we cherish this day.

Our day of birth is unique,
And as we approach another year,
With knowledge gained, we grow,
As a blossom, bloom, so dear.

With a surge of happiness,
We overcome the blues of yesterday.
With a smile and a tear,
We wash away the past, whatever we fear.

Andrina! My wish for you,
Is to hold on to the Iron Rod,
Enjoy your birthday,
And love your God!

Look and See

By
Joseph DeStasio Sr.

"My Son!" Dad would say,
"Life isn't something simple,
Life is a challenge,
A trial, a test.

"As the break of dawn appears,
A new day is born,
A shedding of darkness and fears,
An awakening of hope anew.

"Nay, heed not ill advice.
Lend not thine ears,
To the wasters,
But do, to kindly peers.

"Thou hast trod winter, spring, and fall.
Thou hast walked and walked.
Hast, thou lifted thine eyes?
Hast, thou seen all?

"Beauty is that which surrounds us.
All that God has given,
Will not for naught be.
Should we not look and see?

"Hear me now, oh foolish one,
As we approach another day.
Hear me out and listen;

Listen to what I have to say.

"As sure as the moon gives light,
And the sun's rays bring warmth,
What must be, must be right,
Else all will be in default.

"To smile in all sincerity is bliss.
To frown and doubt is not.
To be certain your reasonings are not amiss,
Be kind, gentle and with goodness fraught."

So Long

By
Joseph DeStasio Sr.
Undated

I've waited so long for you to return,
And now the time is near.
I've waited so long to see you again,
And soon you will be here.

It's been so long since I've seen you,
But my memory of you is clear.
It's almost like you never left,
And that you've always been here.

There wasn't time to get to know you,
Before you went away.
But now that you're coming back,
I won't waste a single day.

I thought I'd soon forget you,
That someone else would take your place,
But when I look at someone else,
I can only remember your face.

Every time I found someone new,
It didn't last for long.
Every time I found a replacement,
I found out I was wrong.

Soon I gave up trying,
To find someone brand new.
Then I realized there was only one for me,
And that only one was you!

Autumn

By
Joseph DeStasio Sr.

July 1948

When green leaves fade, and down do fall,
And discerning breeze is once more near,
Then tis a sign of autumn's call,
With a bid farewell to another year.

Cloaking the earth as they descend
In a blanket of warmth, piling high,
From green to gold, with but one trend,
To bring good cheer and multiply.

The art of nature, realistic and true,
Brings forth joy of amazing wonder.
Certain as the color of the sky so blue,
Sure of light and following thunder.

Spreading relief to a blistering earth,
Serene and calm, unlike an omen,
Finding its way, makes its berth,
For here once more is autumn.

I Love You

By
Joseph DeStasio Sr.
For Eileen DiStasio—His Daughter
1972

How well I remember,
That wintry night.
The snow-covered streets,
Were really a sight.

From home to the mall,
You and I,
Walked and talked,
Of ways not to fall.

Set as I was,
In religious tradition,
Confused as I am,
In this new transition.

I listened with intent,
To your new found interest,
Of a topic Heaven Sent.
Was this a test?

In any case, my dear,
Investigate I will.
To ask, to seek, to hear,
Just one small sound from the Still.

To that of which you feel,
How can I know it too?
Upon my knees, I will kneel.
Dear Daughter of mine, I love you!

Oh, Jesus, My Lord

By
Joseph DeStasio Sr.
1975

Oh, Jesus, my Lord, I love You so!
You are my Savior, and The Way.
Please, tell me what I need to know.
On bended knees, I humbly pray.

I, who am ever so small,
Great are my wants and needs.
My heart yearns for Thy call.
My soul, for Thy light, pleads.

Through this vast universe,
Created by the Great "I Am,"
Father of all, our Father First,
Through Him, my Lord, Your task began.

The soldiers of Jerusalem swarmed about,
Searching, searching throughout the city,
For Thee, my Lord, when just a tot!
Ere, in themselves, not a sign of pity.

A babe in arms, Thou rested so,
Like mine own children too.
What was to come? Why be they foe?
With evil intent, so many they slew.

With Thy Father's Plan of Perfection in tune,
His choice had long since been,
Satan's final error of destruction and doom,
So, Thee, He chose, my Lord, without sin.

We Are What We Are

By
Joseph DeStasio Sr.
1980

We are what we are,
And not what we wish.
We are what we are,
And not what we dream.
We can be what we wish,
We can be what we dream.
If behind that dream of a wish,
We know who we are.

O, Father, We Pray

By
Joseph DeStasio Sr.
June 1983

O, Father, we pray,
What e'er we do,
What e'er we say,
And e'er we go,

Grant us knowledge,
With wisdom.
Grant us courage,
With determination.

Grant us the privilege
To know Thy Son,
Jesus, the Light,
Of our creation.

Nudge us now and then.
Keep us from the pit.
We need Thine attention,
We need Thy grace, and wit.

Bless us, Dear God,
Father in Heaven.
Bless us this day,
Seven times seven.

Although weak be the flesh,
Thy Spirit within,

Seeks to destroy,
The savage of sin.

We pray, O, God,
And needless to say,
Thou art the Master,
Thine is the way!

I Left My House This Morning

By
Joseph DeStasio Sr.
May 1984

I left my house this morning,
While still half asleep,
Went for my car,
And drove off in a jeep.

As I traveled down the road,
Much to my dismay,
I was sitting on the right,
And going the wrong way.

Jolted by a scream,
I turned about and saw,
A frantic man a running.
In heaven's name, what for?

Still, in partial dreamland,
I drove along the lane,
And much to my surprise,
The man behind me came.

He surely must be ill.
Why does he follow me?
Please, dear heart, be still,
That I may stop and see.

I'll turn around this bend,
And go the other way.

Perhaps his mind will mend,
And let me be, I pray.

Good Heavens! What have I done?
Am I still fast asleep?
Or is that Pete, the mailman,
Hooked onto this jeep?!

Children Of the Primary

By

Joseph DeStasio Sr.

June 1984

Children of the Primary,
So young and so sincere,
Innocent and free,
Trusting with nary a fear.

Giving their all,
Their hearts go out.
Beckoning, beckoning, teacher tall,
"Teach us how we came about."

"Within life's span
We live and learn,
Do what we can,
And Salvation must earn."

"For what purpose are we here?
Why must we live and learn?
Do you really care?
What is your concern?

Help us find the truth.
Guide us as we grow.
For we are today's youth,
And tomorrow's leaders, we know!"

"As teachers true, we have gathered
To set the pace for all of you,
As Jesus said, "Nothing mattered,
But for My sake, Be true."

As ye seek, so shall ye find,

Knowledge of the world today.
It may bring wealth, but unkind,
For heart and soul do pray."

"Heed my word, and teachers too.
Live and learn of my creation.
Earn the right to life anew.
For my word, is your Salvation."

Black = Narration
Blue = Teachers Speaking
Purple = Children Speaking
Red = The Lord Speaking

Tis Sad

By
Joseph DeStasio Sr.
January 14, 1985
Used in a Primary Newsletter

To walk a lonely road,
E'er in this land of much,
To be without abode,
Tis sad, indeed, and such.

To look and not see,
To touch and not feel,
To give and not receive,
Tis sad, indeed, tis sad.

One word, one nod, one beam,
A sign, oh, give me that,
As I trudge this constant stream,
Of dim lit paths, so desolate.

What things ought I to know?
What purpose do I serve?
Roaming this vast sphere so,
Tis sad, indeed, tis sad.

If Thou be, then by what power?
If Ye are, then what are Ye?
If Thy rain can raise a flower,
Then surely, a God, Thou must be.

Alone, I am. Alone I'll be.

107

A mere drifting castaway.
If Thou would, please, hear my plea.
Upon my knees to Thee, I pray.

Oh, Father in Heaven! I see it now.
Thy light! Thy light beckons me!
Oh my, Father, for those who know not,
Tis sad, indeed, tis sad!!

This Olden Tree

By
Joseph DeStasio Sr.
February 2, 1985

The beauty that is cast,
Within this universe, I see.
Incomprehensible and so vast,
Tis a wonder, this Olden Tree.

Though wind and snow,
And ravages of winter,
Batter its frame, ever so,
Tall it stands, ne'er a whimper.

Welcoming all young and old,
A haven tranquil, with new lease.
It's limbs ever eager to unfold,
Extending it's offer of rest and peace.

Through its make-up, a rustle of wind,
Sifts its leaves, to bring forth,
Musical enchantment, and in kind,
An awakening of life, and its worth.

Upon its bow, strong and firm,
God's little creatures settle down.
Chirping their songs and, to affirm,
The cheer of spring again renown.

This Olden Tree, this battered hulk,
Forever standing, straight and true,

Though its tusk be difficult,
Beckons all to a life anew.

To rest by its trunk, oh peaceful bliss,
To taste of its fruit, ever sucrose,
To build of it a heart of solace,
This Olden Tree, sans repose.

Unyielding to the gut of time,
Undaunted bearing its ability,
Proudly standing in majestic prime,
Tis God's gift, this Olden Tree.

The Missionaries

By

Joseph DeStasio Sr.

March 3, 1985

From far and near, they come.
Two by two, they travel on.
Even in their teens, so young,
Brave and true, their purpose strong.

Hither and thither, spreading virtue,
Bringing to all, messages sweet.
Of one mind, tried and true,
Their goal, realistic and discreet.

As they trudge the Unknown Path,
In search of Thine own Iron Rod.
With abounding faith, they pray and fast,
Proclaiming their love for Thee, O God!

E'en in this society of love and hate,
E'en in this place of pestilence,
E'en in this world of unknown fate,
Their quest is that of innocence.

Though ravages of time may surely pass,
Greed of man lingers on,
Destroying all, within the mass,
Of people, all, Mother, Father, Daughter, Son.

And so! On they tread, two by two,
Spreading the Gospel, these Missionaries,
Bringing goodwill and light anew,
These creatures of God, the Missionaries.

Ten

By
Joseph DeStasio Sr.
October 17, 1985

A fleeting moment,
Adrift in time, a child again,
A nostalgic flash, a simmering glow,
A glimpse, a spark, and I am ten.

Those joyful days of yesteryear,
How well I remember when,
To slay a dragon without fear,
Came with ease to a boy of ten.

To think, to dream, to create,
To laugh, to cry, and not refrain,
To be alive, to challenge fate,
That I did, when only ten.

To dare the waters of the lake,
Lacking knowledge of the swimming art,
A perilous combo and yet,
I learned to swim when only ten.

To become the adventurer,
Conqueror of men,
A goal desired, and more,
That is the will of a boy of ten.

113

Happiness

By
Joseph DeStasio Sr.
October 30, 1985

Ever winding upward bound,
Spiraling stars reach out,
Making way for all who quest,
That part of life called happiness.

The capacity to love, we have.
The capacity to care, we have.
The capacity to share, we have.
Why then is happiness amiss?

As we tread the stairs of hope,
Blindly groping in a selfish way,
Uncaring, unsharring, we press,
To gain wealth, prestige, and happiness.

"Tis a breeze," I heard them say,
"Ascend the ladder of success.
Pity not the milksop, nor the castaway,
Think of thee and thy happiness."

O foolish ones, have not thee heard,
To spiral upward to the stars,
Thou need be true, gentle and chaste,
To love, to care, to share. That is happiness!

To All Parents

By

Joseph DeStasio Sr. and Eileen DiStasio-Clark

Undated

"I lend you for a little time,
children of Mine," He said,
"For you to love the while they live,
And mourn for when they're dead."

It may be six or seven years,
Or twenty-two or three,
But will you, 'til I call them back,
Take care of them for Me?

They'll bring their charms to gladden you,
And should their stay be brief,
You'll have their lovely memories,
As solace for your grief.

I cannot promise they will stay,
Since all from Earth return.
But there are lessons taught down there,
I want these children to learn.

I've looked the wide world over,
In my search for teachers true,
And from throngs, which crowd life's lanes
I have selected you!

Now will you give them all your love,
Not think your labor vain,

Nor hate Me when I come to call,
To take the back again?

I fancied that I heard them say,
Dear Lord, Thy will be done!
For all the joy the children shall bring,
Risk of grief they'll run.

We'll shelter them with tenderness,
We'll love them while we may,
And for the happiness that we've known,
Forever grateful stay!

But should the Angels call for them,
Much sooner than we've planned,
We'll brave the bitter grief that comes,
For we will understand.

That to Home, with Thee, we will all return,
To live with Mother and Thee.
And if we do it as Thou taught,
An Eternal Family we all will be!

My Street

By

Joseph DeStasio Sr. and Eileen DiStasio-Clark

December 3, 1985

Barely seven feet wide,
The cobblestones in a jutting maze,
Pierced the crust, one by one,
This wonderous sight, was my street.

Our house stood out with red brick facing,
Enhancing its bottom—marble bright.
A low set curl and majestic frame,
A marvel to be seen, on my street.

To hear the Klippity Klop of the horses' hooves,
Pulling its wagon of milk and such.
Remembering, remembering in reverence sweet,
Barely seven feet wide, this was my street.

My Love

By
Joseph DeStasio Sr.
July 29, 1991
Written for Miriam DeStasio, his wife

My love for you is great!
My love for you is true!
My love is real and free!
You are my love, my mate.

Yesterday has gone, and left,
Sweet memories, and bits of dreams.
Today, vigor renewed, with life anew,
Together undaunted, we cling.

My love for you is still intact,
And waits assent, forever more.
Even as we sealed our pact,
Together we'd be, for many a score.

The vow we made, till death do us part,
Bonded us not, to infinity.
T'was the Temple Sealing, Dear Heart,
Our Eternal Enjoining, yours, and mine, my Love.

118

When I Grow Up

By
Joseph DeStasio Sr.
September, 14, 1992

I love you, Mom. I love you, Dad.
When I grow up to be,
Mature, myself, my own,
You'll be proud and glad.

You have done much for me.
You worried, cared, laughed, and cried,
Washed, fed, and clothed me,
And late at night, tired, you sighed.

I love you, Mom. I love you, Dad.
Always near when in need,
Tending, tending, so sincere,
Even longing my soul to feed.

Though I've finally grown up,
Mom, Dad,
I now must find myself,
I know you'll understand.

How Sweet the Din

By
Joseph DeStasio Sr.
June 15, 1993

The crack of a bat,
The roar of a crowd,
Dogs and sodas,
Popcorn and cracker Jack.

From first to second,
Then third, and home,
Holy Moly! Wow! He's in!
How sweet, how sweet the din!

Carrousels, circling round and round.
Barkers barking just a fin.
Children squealing gleefully so,
How sweet, how sweet the din.

Lions, Tigers, Big Top Tent,
A swing, over three rings,
These are the signs of summer fun.
How sweet, how sweet the din.

Myrtle the Turtle

By

Joseph DeStasio Sr.

Written for Miriam DeStasio—His Wife

July 2001

Myrtle the turtle
Jumped over a hurdle,
Tripped on a stone,
And hurt her dome.

She went to the doctor
For medical help.
The doctor was out,
And Myrtle did pout.

She waited all day,
And half the night.
The doctor never came;
Poor Myrtle was a sight.

The pain in her head
Made her scream.
So, home she went, to bed
Awoke next morn and smiled.
'Twas only a dream.

Hum

By
Joseph DeStasio Sr.
September 27, 2007

As I sit so patiently,
I hear the hum so clear.
The mechanics of things,
A wonderful affair.

In unison, to and fro,
The hum rumbles on.
We seek that which is lost,
Not missed till it's gone.

Though life is sweet,
And sometimes not,
Stumble we will,
Naught a thought of retreat.

Time is of essence.
Time is a flit.
Cherish the day,
And enjoy the hum of it.

This Boy

By
Joseph DeStasio Sr.
October 2, 2007

I see this boy, all smiles.
I see this boy in bloom.
I see this boy so dear,
Naught a worry, nary a care.

As time evolves,
Soon he will find,
Growing up is a must,
A challenge in time.

In this jungle of doubt,
A choice he has to make,
To choose or not,
Which way, which way to take.

To heed the wise is just.
To do otherwise is moot.
I see this boy, I see this boy,
Forsaking all in refute.

I pray that after all
In time he will,
Awaken to righteousness,
And heed the Master's call.

Me, You, Melody

By
Joseph DeStasio Sr. and Eileen DiStasio-Clark
1993

To think, to dream, to wish,
To Hope, to want, to live,
To be!
To know that I am.

I think. I dream, and wish.
Ere'in the day will arrive,
Our wants and need be met,
Lest we fall, and not survive.

The gift of life, a miracle,
The gift of society, shame,
Though ye labor throughout,
Your gift be endless pain.

Hear me out, O little one.
Hear me out, and listen!
Remember the Song of Reverie,
Remember, "Me, You, Melody."

Me, You, Melody, Sweet are the words,
Trials and tribulations, opposite you see,
So, when down trodden and all's at ebb,
Think of me, and you, and melody.

How We Spend the Day

By
Eileen DiStasio-Clark
Undated

A breakfast picnic in the park,
A walk along its trail.
A little rest upon our bench,
To read each other's mail.

Then home for lunch, out on the lawn,
We take our time—no fuss.
We watch the clouds go rolling by.
This day is just for us!

Chess or Checkers, Backgammon too,
That is how we will spend the day.
Maybe make some treats, sweat treats,
While we hang around and play.

We will make dinner special,
Italian—it is you and me,
Then snuggle close and friendly,
To watch a movie on T.V.

Too soon, we will have to say goodnight,
But not without a promise.
I will hug you; you will hug me,
Then end the day with a Dark Chocolate Kiss!

What You Mean to Me

By
Eileen DiStasio-Clark
Written for Joseph DeStasio Sr.—Her Father
Undated

A present makes me happy,
A gift brings me joy,
But nothing in the world,
Could make me feel the way you do.

You put the sunshine in every morning,
Even if it rains.
You make the stars shine bright,
Even when they don't.

I could live without a lot,
Like luxuries and money.
Even loss of limbs or senses,
Wouldn't end my life.

But, Daddy, if you went away,
Then time would stop for me.
Because you see I love you!
Truly! Truly! Truly!

To Grow

By
Eileen DiStasio-Clark
Undated

Although it was gone,
Letting go was not easy.
Memories pulled the heartstrings,
Making life queasy.

But through the dark night
Of struggle and great sorrow,
Comes the miraculous change,
That helps us to grow.

So do not dismay
When life challenges your soul.
God takes the broken pieces,
And fashions a new whole!

Our Twain Shall Meet

By
Eileen DiStasio-Clark
Undated

If never our twain shall meet,
I will have to face defeat,
The end will not be sweet,
If never our twain shall meet,
Surely, our twain shall meet!
There will never be defeat!
Our end will be most sweet!
Surely, our twain shall meet!

To Feel

By
Eileen DiStasio-Clark
Undated

To feel is good,
When you feel good.
But it hurts,
When you hurt,
And that is not good!

Or is it?

To hurt feels bad,
When you feel bad.
But it is growth,
When you grow.
And that is not bad!

The Nature of Life Is Motion

By
Eileen DiStasio-Clark
Undated

The nature of life is motion,
You move forward, climb upward,
Or you slide backward, fall downward,
No one can ever stand still.

Despite your strength and commitment,
If you choose to stay in place,
Great will be the failure you face,
No one can ever stand still.

The nature of life is motion,
Keep moving, going, growing…
Your greatest strength lies in knowing,
No one can ever stand still.

But be sure yours is the right path,
And move forward, climb upward.
Do not slide backward, fall downward,
And never, ever stand still!

Guided

By
Eileen DiStasio-Clark
Undated

The law of opposition,
Makes it very clear,
People have to make one choice,
As long as they are here.

They can choose the good or bad,
Choose the great or small,
But they can choose only one way,
They cannot have it all.

So, in this life it is wisest,
For people must be smart,
To follow, not the mind of man,
But to walk by the Spirit's Heart!

By This I Know I Will Win

By
Eileen DiStasio-Clark
Undated

Deep is my love,
For all that is good.
Full is my commitment,
To doing all that I should.

There will be no amending,
Of any gospel law!
Doctrines will be lived,
Devoid of flaw!

True to counsels,
Principles, commands;
Steadfast, I will remain.
Immoveable, I will stand.

I will make no compromise,
Nor ever fall away!
With Him I will stand,
On judgement Day!

I Win

By
Eileen DiStasio-Clark
Composed while chasing flies.
Undated

I WIN!
I always do!
You are fast,
But I am bigger than you!
You are the bug,
I am the boss!
No one is going,
To mourn your loss!

Sad Day Sonnet

By
Eileen DiStasio-Clark
2002

It's not that I have questions,
It's not that I've lost hope,
It's just that situations,
Make it hard to cope.

To know that he once loved me,
And feel his distance now,
It to burn with the frostbite,
Of a broken vow.

To remember what we had,
Have nothing 'tween us here,
Is to bleed away life's hope,
Pierced by Satan's spear.

I know that Satan hates me,
He messes up my life,
Muddling the good days,
Mixing them with strife.

He pressures me to question
The things I know are true.
Not about the gospel, but
About me and you.

He tells me, "You're always wrong!"
He always interferes,

Pestering with confusions,
Bringing me to tears.

Of course, it does not pain me,
To know I'm not his friend.
I just wish he'd go away,
Let my poor heart mend.

I wish he'd lose my number,
And forget where I live,
Not make me guest of honor,
At parties he gives.

But I will never give up!
I will wait my life through,
Until the Spirit tells me,
Who stands in place of you!

So, I can expect Satan,
To pursue his dark goal,
Of mincing up my peace,
Rumbling my soul.

But he will fight me in vain,
For I will never choose,
To make truth of his lies.
Surely, he will lose!

If You Would Let Me Teach You

By
Eileen DiStasio-Clark
February 2, 2007
About Life Before We Were Born

If you would let me teach you,
I would enlighten your minds
with truths—eternal,
with knowledge of worth,
with principles divine.

I would teach you about God
—Our Father and Mother—
of kinship
in Their family,
as sisters and brothers,

of the worth that we possess
as the children of a God,
of our yearning
to be as They are,
to walk the path They trod.

I would teach you of the world
in which we lived pre-mortal,
when a plan was laid
to save our souls—
open Godhood's portal.

Where, with agency possessed

as a rightful attribute,
we were free to choose,
when the war began,
which leader we would salute.

About How This Life Began

If you would let me teach you,
I would speak to your spirits,
reminding of things
you knew long ago,
sharing them bit by bit.

I would teach you of this world,
and why it was created,
of the sacred laws
and covenants which
were, for us, instated,

of elements commanded,
and of chaos organized,
of form and beauty,
of abundant life,
and nature's laws devised,

of the Garden called Eden,
of Adam and his wife, Eve,
of their temptation,
the Adversary,
and why they had to leave.

I would teach you of mortal life,
how this is a probation,
with tests and trials,
and time that is measured:
prep for exaltation.

The Veil of Forgetfulness,

the great purpose of the fall,
and opposition
would be explained,
so you would understand them all.

That there is pain and sickness,
that we must work and travail,
you will come to know
are not punishments;
they help us to prevail.

About How It All Worked Out

If you would let me teach you,
I would whisper to your hearts
of virtues—holy,
attributes—noble,
talents—the golden parts.

I would teach you of the Savior
—our Brother, Lord, and Friend—
of His Virgin Birth,
His life and mission,
and of His mortal end.

The prophecies about Him,
is the point where we would begin:
how they were fulfilled,
the path that He paved,
His life, lived without sin.

You would learn of His oppressors,
why they persecuted Him,
and of the humble,
who followed His Light,
which never has gone dim,

of the torment He endured
to balance the books of sin,
the key He turned to
unlock heaven's gates,
that we may enter in,

why the rising of the Son
is important to us all,
how it gives us means
to achieve the goal
that was threatened by the fall.

You would come to understand
that the sacrament reminds
of the life and blood
that was shed for us,
how us to Him it binds.

You would also come to know
that the Savior did provide
a way by which we
could connect with Him:
The Dove was sent as guide.

I would teach of the darkness
cast by the death of the Son,
how the truth was lost
through Apostasy,
why Satan thought he had won,

of the Demon's black designs
to shroud, with philosophies,
the exalting truths
that would prepare us
for the Eternities.

I would teach of other worlds

in which we have yet to dwell,
the two divides of
the post-mortal realm:
Paradise or Heaven, Prison or Hell.

The prices of admission,
and the things those tickets buy,
you would understand
must be paid for here,
in full, before we die.

That realm is like the chambers
where we prepare the cases
we will present to God
at the judgment bar—
temporary places.

About What Is to Come

If you would let me teach you,
I would help you to prepare
for the Lord's return,
so, you would be ready
the day that He gets here.

I would teach of the chaos
that will abound before He comes,
of the signs by which
you would know the beating
of Armageddon's drums,

of political unrest,
of moral conflagration,
of seasons confused,
economic woe,
and strife between nations,

of the Zion we will build,
of its uniting order,
of prosperity,
peace, and joy that we will
find within its borders.

I would teach you of the day
that the Savior will return,
how a world at war
will be quieted,
and receive what it earned,

of the council He will hold
at Adam—Ondi—Ahman,

to receive what is His
—the Keys Eternal—
from those who have held them,

of the visit He will make
to His house on Zion's hill,
of how none will know
but the few prepared,
who have learned and done His will.

We will talk of His arrival
at the height of contention,
when all will confess,
and may repent,
before the great destruction.

About The Millenium

If you would let me teach you,
I would open to your views
the truths about the
Millennium that
will afterwards ensue.
I would teach of temples,
of how they will fill the earth,
of peace and goodness
—For a thousand years—
Devoid of dross and dearth,

when all the world will be one,
—united—in harmony—
self-governed under
the Lord, our King,
unbound eternally.

About The Final Restoration

If you would let me teach you,
I would show you where to find
that unknown "something"
for which you once searched,
but never could define.

I would teach restoration
—tell you why we needed one—
lest you should believe
truth changed over time,
or that God's work is done.

You would learn about the prophets
through whom all things were restored,
of apostles and
of missionaries
who work under the Lord.

The gift of revelation,
Holy Scriptures, old and new,
would testify,
to your mind and heart,
that all these things are true.

I would teach what Jesus taught
—effective, humble prayer—
to bring you close to
Father, to receive
His promises and care.

Faith and hope and trusting God,

regarding Him with honor,
the role of the fast
in uniting us with Him,
again, and evermore.

Sacrifice would be defined.
We would talk of charity,
of love and service,
of selflessness, and
how they bless families.

You would come to understand
the family's supreme role,
why parenthood, in
eternal union,
is the noblest goal,

of the law of chastity,
and the sanctity of life,
we would talk, at length,
and enumerate
the joy with which they are rife.

Courage would be highlighted,
obedience, underscored,
for they are major
in life's symphony,
an elemental chord.

We would dwell upon commandments,
and the patience that we need
to endure this life,
in humility,

to follow the Lord's lead.

Repentance and forgiveness
would be lessons we would not miss,
for they are crucial
—the platinum keys—
to mortal happiness.

You would learn of temple work,
and family histories,
of ordinances
and of all the things
that had been mysteries.

About The Final Battle

If you would let me teach you,
I would expand your visions
far beyond the scope
and the limits of
your educated ones.

I would explain the battle
that Magog and Gog will fight,
the final conflict
between good and evil
between Darkness and the Light.

The war—begun pre-mortal—
and waged by the Morning's Son,
will be decided
on that dreadful day,
and the right will have won!

About the Eternal Worlds

If you would let me teach you,
I would magnify your kens
with the knowledge of
the eternal worlds
awaiting mortal men.

I would speak of the darkness
which awaits Perdition's sons,
who earned no glory,
nor kingdom of light—
they are the evil ones.

You would learn of the starry realm
inherited by the weak,
who willingly chose
to reject the truth,
the sinful—so to speak,

and of the lunar kingdom,
prepared for the good of heart,
who sought no one's hurt,
did little wrong, but
did no more than their part,

of the kingdom of the sun
where the valiant will go,
those who were righteous
beyond measure,
who sought—their God—to know.

of those who will be crowned with glory

adorned in Deity's robes;
for through sorrow and
joy they endured, like
the Joseph's and the Jobs.

About This Life's Experiences

If you would let me teach you
I would most willingly share
the knowledge I have
of the choices we chose,
of which you are unaware.

I would testify to you
of that choice we chose to make,
and that, on this journey
through mortality,
your commitment you would not forsake.

Because you do not remember
life in our former sphere,
you would disbelieve,
and question the truth,
of the promises you all made there.

Still, I would try to teach you
—as I know that I did then—
of God's plan for man
with its treasure rich—
teach it to you again.

I would help you to recall
the way that you had been,
your love of truth, and
desire to learn,
your aversion to sin.

I would tell you about me,
and my passion for the truth,
how I loved to teach,
and defend the weak,
the things that brought me ruth.

I would tell you how we met
—as well as I can recall—
why the time we shared
all with each other
was among the best times of them all,

about how all of you were drawn to me,
for reasons hard to explain,
from back of the group,
to right by my side,
to learn, there you chose to remain,

about how I welcomed all of you,
for reasons, I could not express,
and how teaching you,
brought a joy that felt like a
spiritual caress.

Though you would be skeptical
about anything I would say,
I would reminisce about
the walks we took, and
the talks along the way.

I would share what I remember
of how our friendships grew
from acquaintances, small,

to friendships, strong,
deep friendships, dear and true,

of how we learned together
about truth, and that you and me,
are brothers and sisters
inseparable—
as close as friends could be,

of our keen desires
to learn and grow together,
what we would need to do,
to all return Home
to Father and Mother.

I would speak of the commitments,
our determinations true,
your promises to me
to live by the truth,
the promises I made to all of you,

to petition to our Father
for Him, His assistance to wield;
His approval and
His cautions about
the dangers life would yield,

that there would be many choices,
how He had told us to take care,
for what we did or
did not do there, would make
all the difference here.

I am sure that some of you would question,

the good of a life forgot.
Love not remembered,
promise not recalled,
would be to you as naught.

Still, I would tell you about
the expectations we had
to meet again and
help one another,
through the good times and bad,

of Father's promise to help,
so, we would know what to choose;
though the choices would
be ours to make—
He would send the Dove with clues.

I would describe your eagerness
to partake of mortal life,
and your excitement
to try many things,
gleaning strengths from your strife.

I would tell how, with confidence,
you all left with commitment, strong,
knowing you would have
to struggle, but not
believing you would go wrong,

how we knew from life's trials,
we would not think to cower,
though some of you knew not that
you did not know, the

strength of Satan's power,

how not all did not understand,
though we knew we could prevail,
what life would be like
without former ken,
living under the veil.

Since you have closed your minds to
everything religious,
it is not likely
that you could be moved
just by what has been given us.

So, I would clarify how,
that which drew us together,
keeps me bound to all of you,
connected with a
spiritual tether.

Though we may have been equal
in knowledge and commitment,
we were not in strength or
understanding, and
we did know what that meant.

Your intents were to excel,
to rise above the Tempter,
overcome this world,
gain the great reward,
return Home forever.

But we knew there would be dangers
everyone would have to face.

Temptations, trials
and oppositions
make this a risky place.

With eye singled to glory,
I knew that I would not stray.
But your sights were broad
and I worried that
within this life, some of you would stray.

We would all live in separate places
through the years of childhood,
but the time and space
that severed us, was
meant to serve our good.

Because many of you strongly embraced
the philosophies of man,
and have lost your faith
in God's simple truth,
you do not understand

that all things have a purpose—
but only one road can lead us Home—
if we will follow
the correct signposts
and the guides; should we roam.

I would help you remember
the promises you each made with me,
to be good and strong
so that we could stay
in The Eternal Family.

I would restate my solemn vow
to search until I found you,
to bring you back home,
if you had wandered—
forever to be true.

You would learn, the length of parting
was not something that we knew,
for the space of time
would be determined
by what we chose to do.

There was possibility
that we could lose each other,
but we had promised
to be loyal and true
forever Sisters and Brothers.

We did not all come together;
Each one of us had our day.
For we had questions for
Father, and
He had much to say.

Now, if your minds are narrow
you would only be amused
by the concepts that
I would share with you, but
they cannot be excused.

I would testify to you;
their significance is great,
for they effect the

outcome of our
final, eternal fate.

You would learn that, before we left,
we sought a confirmation
that there would be a
day of reunion,
of joy and elation.

I would list Father's promises:
He would direct and urge aright,
He would guide us toward
our chosen end,
He would lead us through the night,

He would provide the way by which
we could achieve our goal,
the gospel truths
would be given us;
they would save the obedient soul.

I would confess I did not know
how all things would be worked out,
nor that the course of
my life's journey would
need an alternate route.

I would explain how I felt
when I learned "my friends" were you,
how my heart was wrenched,
my mind confused, and
my spirit's cast turned blue.

Though I know you have closed your minds
to the truth you were taught there;
and you have closed your hearts
to the choices you made,
and you no longer care,

I cannot walk away from you,
nor leave my friends behind;
I need to know why
things are as they are;
I need, some peace, to find.

"Why, sooner, did we not meet,
did we not grow together;
and why had you not
received the gospel
to make your lives better?"

These were the questions I asked.
Through Groban, Father replied.
Though the answer was
quite simple; as I
listened, my spirit cried.

The adventure of this life
was a siren to your souls.
The achievement of
its holy purpose
was not your only goal.

You sought to partake of meats,
to swim in its trepid seas.
I would have had you

164

taste of its fruits, and
sail with a gentle breeze.

You all needed to "go alone"
so your choices would be yours.
You all needed to know
that when you anchored,
it was you, choosing the shores.

You have barred me from your souls,
built a wall around your hearts.
You push me away,
and you stand afar,
of your lives, I have no part.

For there were to be no "what ifs."
There were to be no "maybes."
As truth is told, you
have marked your own courses,
and left me with queries.

For there were—no doubt—those times
when angels prompted choices,
which would have let me
help you sooner,
if you had heard those voices.

But to a different drum
some of you marched in disharmony,
living lives that
distorted your views—
put you at odds with me.

So, I am asking Father,

165

"How can I help them to see?"
"Will they seek glory,
as they did afore?
"Will they 'reach out to Thee?'"

"Will they let me teach them of Thee?"
"Or will they, from Thee always roam?"
"Will they 'take Thy hand?'"
"Will they 'call Thy name?'"
"Will they choose to 'come Home?'"

These are the things I would share
if you would let me teach you.
There must be a way,
to return to you
all of these things you knew!

About the Questions We All Asked

If you would let me teach you,
I would enlighten your minds,
speak to your spirits,
whisper to your heart,
would show you where to find,

the answers to the questions
proposed by everyone:
"From where did I come,
And why am I here?"
"Where go I, when life is done?"
I would expand your visions.
I would help you to prepare,
open to your views,
magnify your kens,
would most willingly share

the only truths that matter,
that explicate life's purpose,
so you all may obtain
what you chose afore—
glory—tendered to us.

Silence Is Not Always Golden

By
Eileen DiStasio-Clark
February 23, 2017

They say that silence is golden,
And while that may, in some ways, be true,
When applied in place of expression,
It becomes something you may rue.

For silence is words unspoken,
The letter unwritten, the text not sent,
Expressing a powerful message,
That you may or may not have meant.

So, give silence a little space,
While remembering that keeping things real,
Requires adequate expression
To show how you honestly feel.

Returning Back Home

By
Eileen DiStasio-Clark
February 23, 2017

Jehovah, I am returning!
I love Thee!
I miss Thee!
I want to always be with Thee!
I am returning!

Mother, I am coming back!
I love Thee!
I miss Thee!
I wanted to remain by Thee!
I am coming back!

Father, I am coming Home!
I love Thee!
I miss Thee!
I never wanted to leave Thee!
I am coming Home!

You Will Win!

By
Eileen DiStasio-Clark
2017

Do not give up…
Do not give in…
Turn to God,
And you will win,
Both the Race,
And a place,
In God's Hall of Fame!

Beyond My Own

By
Eileen DiStasio-Clark
January 2018

Once upon a time ago,
When all my kids were home,
I was busy as could be;
There was no time alone!

Now that life has changed for me,
I see I am not too good,
At being by myself so much;
So, I decided that I would…

Extend my love and blessings,
Beyond my own, this year;
You are the family I chose,
With whom I want to share.

So let us begin as Family—
And focus on together;
Here are some things for planning and play,
You may do with them… whatever.

You do yours and I will do mine,
Then in Their Heavenly Books,
Angels will record for us,
How our friendship looks.

Conductor's Welcome

By

Eileen DiStasio-Clark

February 2018

Written for the Opening Greeting of Family Home Evening

C is for Climbing; let us make it Jacob's Ladder.

O is for Obedience to the laws that really matter.

N is for the Nothing that we will let get in our way, as we seek
to
make right choices, in all things, every day!

D is for Devotion; it tightens our grip on The Rod.

U is for Understanding, the kind that comes from God.

C is for Celestial Glory, the reward for righteous living.

T is for Tests of Life and the growth they continue giving.

O is for Obstacles Satan places in our path.

R is for Repentance; it keeps us eligible for what God hath.

S is for Savior; His teachings, life, and love that promise us
the
glory testified of, by the Dove!

W is for Worldliness; leave it alone; from it run!

E is for the good Example we must set for everyone.

L is for Longsuffering; and a never-ending trust.

C is for Commandments, the only laws that are truly just.

O is for Ordinances; they bind us to our God.

M is for His Miracles that help us beat the odds.

E is for Exaltation, the goal for which we strive.

In fact, it is the reason that we are all alive.
Now this may sound kind of silly;
The grammar is a bit dumb,
Nevertheless, dear Family,
It is my Conductor's Welcome!!

What Never Giving Up Looks Like to Me

By
Eileen DiStasio-Clark
2023

A massive ark, constructed from wood
Fallen from a dead tree, and rotted.
Lined with pitch collected from birch,
Not smoothed on, just dotted.

I fix and repair.
I take very good car…
As I travel across the sea;
I WILL reach my Eternal Destiny.

Tossed, submerged, and blown by the winds
That howl with a raging voice that dins.
Bolts of lightning and thundering air currents
Present as nature's relentless deterrents.

I proceed and persist,
Wrong turns I resist,
As I travel across the sea;
I WILL reach my Eternal Destiny.

On deck, at the helm, alone, without crew
No light from the sky, nor map to review,
Mountains and valleys creep up from the deep,
From all things good threatening to keep.

I look beyond the view,
I radio YOU
As I travel across the sea,
I WILL reach my Eternal Destiny.

www.ingramcontent.com/pod-product-compliance
Lightning Source LLC
Chambersburg PA
CBHW071744120626
46550CB00002B/659